Next Point Wins

NEXT POINT WINS

A Playbook for Future Champions

by

Coach Dave Gray

ISBN 978-1-960378-38-5   (paperback)
ISBN 978-1-960378-39-2   (ePub)

First Edition

Published in collaboration with Ascender Book Services
www.ascenderbook.services

Book design by Anna Hall

CONTENTS

INTRODUCTION

Coach, Do You Remember Me?

During the school year, I sometimes run a program called Recess Buddies. This program has been more than just a fun way to connect with kids outside of the gym. Those kids, in that setting, have taught me one of the most important lessons I've learned in over twenty-five years of coaching.

One of my personal goals is to always make every individual I engage with feel like an MVP (Most Valuable Person). The plan for that first day of Recess Buddies was to seek out those children who aren't as quick to get involved in games, activities, and social interaction at school and find ways to make them feel like an MVP in front of their peers.

I learned quickly that the MVP plan would have to wait until I could get everyone calmed down. Many of these kids were familiar with me from past camps, leagues, events, and school assemblies. The second they spotted me on the playground, it was chaos.

"Coach Dave, I can't believe you're at our school."

"Hey, Coach Dave, let's play soccer!"

"No, flag football!"

"I want to play Wiffle Ball!"

"Coach Dave, are you just doing this one recess, or can you be here for every recess?"

So far, at least the program had succeeded in making me feel like an MVP.

But the profound lesson is what came next. Over the course of five recesses, many of the children who knew me prior to Recess Buddies would run up and ask some variation of the same question: "Coach Dave, do you remember me?"

They would want to know if I remembered their name. Or the nickname I gave them in camp last summer. Or if I remembered the time they made this one great play in a game I was coaching.

"Do you remember me?"

Through that question, asked over and over again, I learned that one of the biggest needs for every child is to *be recognized*. Seen. Remembered. They need to know that they're significant, that they play a role in this world, and that they matter. For children and adolescents, the need is as essential as sleep, exercise, and even love. And unfortunately, in today's world, too many are seeing this need go unfulfilled.

I See You

I'm five years old, and my parents are visiting me on a Sunday at the home of the foster family I've been staying with. My father is battling the disease of alcoholism, so my biological parents are not equipped to raise me at this time. This will be the first of many stops through an early childhood spent bouncing between foster families and extended family members who make the incredibly selfless decision to take me in whenever they can.

"We have to go now," I can still hear my mother saying.

At that age, being so new to the idea of foster care, I can't understand why my parents have sent me to this house. Or why they can only come visit me on weekends. I love my mother. And my father, no matter what he's going through, is my hero.

"Why do I have to stay here?" I ask. "Why can't I go with you?"

"There's going to come a time when you can be with us," my father tries to explain.

And then they get up to leave. My foster family isn't there to stop me, so I run after my mom and dad as they head out to the car. One of my most vivid childhood memories is of the long country road leading away from my foster family's house, the car kicking up dust as my parents take off.

"No!" I cry out. "Take me with you."

I chase them down the dirt road, screaming after them all the way, until I can't run any farther.

Every time they visit—and they will visit faithfully every week—it's the same. I beg them to take me with them. "Why can't I go home with you? Why can't I live with you?" They leave me behind the same way every time, and every time, I chase after them, running and screaming until I collapse. Then, I wait there at the end of the road until I finally calm down because I don't want my foster family to see me crying.

Why, out of all my childhood memories, does this one stand out the strongest? It was intensely emotional, of course, but I think it runs deeper than that. It stands out to me because it's the clearest example of a time from my childhood when I wasn't having that fundamental need fulfilled.

I felt like I didn't matter. Like no one saw me.

I spent my whole life wanting to be seen. The mistakes I've made were because I wanted to be seen. Any accomplishments, any developments of my skillset, every moment where

I came closer to finding my passion, every measure of my ability to empathize with and connect with children—it all stems from the fact that I have lived it and can truly see this part of their journey. The struggle was so real, so prolonged, and so intense for me that I can always put myself back there.

Though the words "I see you" can be as impactful as "I love you," it isn't enough to simply speak the words. The *actions* you take must also make it clear that you see the child or adolescent, you recognize who they are, and that you value them.

Eighteen Inches

At recess, there's a pecking order. If you give children that kind of freedom, they're going to separate into groups. Some children are going to be left out of these groups. On any playground in the world, there will always be students hanging on the edges of the action, keeping to themselves while their peers play their games. I know this not just because of Recess Buddies, or because of my twenty-five-plus years of coaching and working with children, but because there was a time in my life when I was one of them.

So, for me, Recess Buddies served as a challenge to reach these kids. This is a difficult thing to do effectively. I didn't want to put them in an awkward position by calling out to them and saying, "Hey, I see you're not playing. Why don't you get in there?" There's a fine line between helping a young person feel as if they are genuinely being included with the group and making them feel as if they are being singled out for ridicule.

The most effective way to stay on the right side of that line is to show them that you see them.

"Hey, my name is Coach Dave. What's your name? How's your day going?"

A simple approach designed to show them that you want to know who they are—that's such a powerful way to make them feel included. You have to *see* them first, and then you have to *demonstrate* that you see them.[1] And this doesn't just apply to the children who don't readily join in group activities. This applies to every child. If you want to connect with them, then you first have to make it clear that you see them and understand them.

In the chapters to come, I share lessons learned from a lifetime of coaching and connecting with young people. While this book can serve as a guide for coaches, teachers, and parents hoping to reach children on a new level, its deeper purpose is to equip young people with the lessons they need to connect with others. Think of it as something like a *How to Win Friends and Influence People* for kids. For the adults reading this book, the lessons will help you explore how to recognize and validate the young people in your life; how to listen and ask questions; how to give positive reinforcement; how to avoid social comparisons and judgment; how to be mindful of body language, tone, and inflection; how to be truthful and consistent; how to give of our *time*, which is one of the greatest gifts we can give; and above all, how to view coaching/teaching/parenting through the lens of a child.

---

1   Every young person is different, of course, so this approach doesn't work for everyone. At Recess Buddies, and in any program I've ever hosted, there are always one or two children who keep their guard up, who just walk away and don't want to interact. But every so often, you get to enjoy a little victory. Every so often, one of these kids will open up, join in the game (if only for a little while), and even start to talk and interact with his or her peers. When that happens, it's nothing short of magical.

For the young people reading this book, you will find strategies to help you shape your unique identity. You will also learn how to develop positive self talk; how to avoid judgment; how to live with empathy, authenticity, and honesty; how to be a good listener and friend; how to be responsible and accountable; how to show enthusiasm; and how to take the initiative in your life.

But before we do any of that, it's important to build that foundation for everything to come. That foundation is this first lesson about the importance of "I see you." Making the people you meet recognize that you see and understand them is such a powerful thing. It's the key to unlocking your ability to connect not just with young people, but with anyone. You have to see them, and just as importantly, you have to find ways to make them *know* that you see them.

When you begin to think about that fundamental need to be seen and understood, it changes almost everything about your mindset. Treating other people in a way that shows them you see them fulfills that same need for you to be seen. It becomes a perpetual cycle of positivity. This is why I do so many of my programs like Recess Buddies pro bono. It has become my purpose to let parents, coaches, teachers, administrators, and young people recognize that I see them. They do so in return, and that energy and enthusiasm is all I need to keep myself going.

There's a visual I use in some of my assemblies and pep talks that illustrates the physical distance between a person's brain and heart. On average, that distance is eighteen inches. With this illustration, I make the point that it's not enough to simply hear and think about a new lesson. If it's going to be effective—if it's really going to lead to growth and change in your life—then the lesson has to travel those eighteen inches of distance between your brain and your heart. You can't just hear it; you have to internalize it. Make it a part of who you are and what you stand for.

When it comes to our first big lesson, "I see you," it's about taking action, and doing so from the heart. Don't just tell kids you see them; show them how you see them and why you see them. Do this, and you will instill confidence and self-esteem in the child. They will start to believe in themselves, build on this feeling, and grow and learn toward a better version of themselves.

The Playbook

I've always been a coach at heart, so each chapter to come will be presented like a playbook of sorts—a play-by-play guide that young people can use to help these lessons travel the eighteen inches to where they become internalized. While this playbook is designed for children and adolescents, it is certainly something that adults can use as well, and it is particularly effective when the parent or guardian learns them together with the young person in their life.

All of this is going to take discovery. We have a journey before us. The playbook will serve as a guide, and also as a series of actionable steps, but we as the adults on the journey have to lead by example. If the young people in our lives are going to meet with success in any of this, we have to demonstrate how it's done. It isn't enough to just teach and preach; we have to portray these principles ourselves. We have to walk the walk. If we can do this, then the kids will follow.

The most satisfying phenomenon I have witnessed in my career coaching young people is that when they start to live these lessons, they don't simply use them to better themselves. They spread their positivity to the other people in their lives. That positivity becomes more than just their own habit; it becomes a habit for their friends and family. By example, they teach others. The cycle of positivity only grows.

In this way, I didn't just write this book for you or the child or adolescent in your care. It's not just for one or two people to learn how to be the best person they can be. This book is intended to serve as a call to action that causes a ripple effect. If we can all work together to make the young person reading this the best person he/she can be, then that empowers him or her to help others be the best they can be.

Ultimately, the change this book seeks is not just in you or the people you care about. In a world full of increasing divisions, perceived differences, and cultural isolation, this book seeks to positively impact our culture, our community, and our society.

The Light Shines Inside All of Us

I remember this kid who spent the first seven years of his childhood living in foster homes and with extended family members, until his aunt and uncle made the loving, selfless decision to become his legal guardians. This kid loved his mother and father more than anything, and he couldn't understand at the time why he couldn't be raised by them.

I remember this kid who was placed in remedial learning programs in elementary school because of perceived behavioral and emotional disabilities. This kid was bullied so badly on the school bus, he was forced to use his saxophone case as a seat in the middle aisle because no one would let him sit with them. He had no drive or motivation to excel in school, or even to be anything better than a *C* student.

I remember this kid who dropped out of college after two years and was kicked out of the house at eighteen years old.

I remember this kid who worked menial jobs to scrape by, barely making ends meet. It seemed like he could never quite find his identity and purpose in life.

I remember this kid. I know this kid. This kid is me.

When I think back on this kid, I remember that he also never gave up on himself. He knew deep, deep down inside that one day, he would have something positive and meaningful to share with the world.

You see, through all the adversity and challenges in my childhood/adolescent years, I had this flickering light inside of me—kind of like a pilot light. I believe every child has inside of them a flickering light that has potential to be as big and shine as bright as a lighthouse.

There are countless kids out there going through their own painful situations right now. Some are feeling left behind or left out completely. Some wear their heart on their sleeve, and we can easily identify that they're hurting. Others hide or disguise the hurt within to where no one would know. I am a walking, talking, coaching, bright, beaming, shining lighthouse today because someone noticed my flickering light. Someone told me I was significant. Someone told me that I mattered.

So that's a huge part of what we're going to be doing with this book: We're going to look closely for the flickering light. It's sometimes hard to see under the fear, negativity, and self-doubt that many young people carry with them. But as a person who works with those same young people every day, I can tell you for a fact that it doesn't have to be this way.

For you, as a young person reading this, it's just a matter of putting in the work to change your mindset to where you think more positively. All the tools to do that are included in the Chalk Talks to come.

And if you're an adult reading this, it's important to know that the young people in your life want to hear you say that they are significant, and they really do matter. More importantly, they want you to *show* them how they matter. I know I wanted this in my own life. It's why I made youth coaching a career.

Now, back to the kids. This is my message to you as we move forward with our Chalk Talks: Don't give up, don't lose hope, never stop believing in your potential. Stay in the game. My flickering light became a lighthouse . . . Yours will too!

CHALK TALK #1

Character Is Your Most Important Piece of Equipment

Ability may get you to the top, but it takes character to keep you there.

–John Wooden

In the championship game of a youth flag football league, a twelve-year-old named Johnny changed everything I thought I knew about what it means to have strong character.

The adults on the sidelines don't do any of the play calling in this league. We leave that up to the kids on the field. The play that Johnny called for his defense when his team broke the huddle is one I'll never forget. The other team was driving down the field in a tie game, and a touchdown might have made the difference between winning and losing.

After a time-out, I blew the whistle as the referee, and the teams broke into their formations. The team on offense handed the ball off to Charlie, who happens to have a physical disability. Charlie must not have been expecting to get the ball, because he stood there and stared at it with wide eyes for a second.

"Go, Charlie!" everyone started cheering. "Run, run, run!" Charlie took off.

Each kid on Johnny's defense went after Charlie's flags, but they always made sure to miss. Charlie would stop to check that he still had his flags, then take off again. Johnny and all the other defenders kept lunging for him, getting their hands on his flags before letting them slip through their fingers.

When Charlie crossed into the end zone, every player on both teams celebrated like he had just won the Super Bowl. It was Charlie's only touchdown of the season.

I don't remember who won that game. Probably none of the kids or adults do either. But everyone remembers that play. Not just because it meant the world to Charlie, but because it said something about Johnny's character. The reason he had called time-out was because he had a feeling that Charlie would get the ball. And what he told his teammates had nothing to do with stopping the offense and winning the game. He told them to let Charlie score, to make it look like they were doing everything they could to stop him, and most importantly, to celebrate with him after he scored.

Johnny had the strong character to set aside his competitive nature and give Charlie something that meant the world to him. In just one moment, Johnny showed how your accomplishments are a part of character, but they are not even close to the biggest part. The biggest part? It's all about what you *do for other people.*

In this book, we're going to talk about the kinds of things you can do to help you with just about every part of your life—in school, with friends, in your after-school activities, at home. But it all starts with your character. Your character is the foundation of who you are. It's your most important piece of equipment.

So, how do we make sure that your most important piece of equipment is as strong as it can be? Here's the playbook:

CHARACTER
IS YOUR BEST PIECE
OF EQUIPMENT

1. Find Your Superpower.

If you know me, then it might surprise you to learn that, when I was a kid, I was shy and timid. I wasn't always so outgoing and enthusiastic. On top of that, I wore these Coke-bottle glasses, my clothes weren't always the best, and I definitely could have taken better care of my hair. But here's the thing about me as a kid: I also felt like I had more potential to unlock in myself. I liked the sound of my name, and I knew that my personality could get me somewhere as long as I let it.

There's one thing I know for a fact to be true about everyone, no matter who they are: They have a superpower. They just need to figure out how to unlock it. For me, I eventually learned that my superpower was my ability to remember important details about everyone I met, including their names. By the time I got to high school, a habit had formed. Every day, I would go around shaking people's hands, saying good morning, and using everyone's name.

Just like at any school, most of the other kids would only hang out with the friends in their own little circles. But because of my willingness to show kindness, genuine interest, and courtesy, each group took me in as part of their own. I wasn't doing this just so I could be popular and feel accepted by the other kids in school either. My superpower was that I genuinely cared about everyone. And I learned through practice that people respond to that kind of thing.

No matter who you are, you have a superpower. I can't tell you for certain what it is—that's up to you to figure out—but what I *can* tell you is that everyone, no matter what their main superpower happens to be, has a *second* superpower that they can choose to use or not. That superpower is *kindness*. You might have noticed that in the story about me in high school,

I used my superpower to make people feel better about themselves. I combined my ability to remember details about the people I met with a desire to be kind to those people.

In your life, you will meet people who are kind to you. These people will make a huge impact on who you are. As a kid, it's important to recognize these people when they come into your life. At the same time, even as a kid, you should try to be that person to someone else. Someone who has strong character will go out of their way to be kind to the people in their life. We all know this, but not enough of us think about ways to make kindness an active part of how we live each day.

Before we start thinking about how to make this first play a part of who you are, and before we learn any more plays, I want to call us back to an idea from the introduction to this book. This way, if you didn't read the introduction, then we can begin to internalize the idea right here in the first Chalk Talk. Here it is: For the average person, the distance between the brain and the heart is only about eighteen inches. Think about that. Just eighteen inches.

Why do I bring this up? Because if you read all the messages in this book—if you read every single word from cover to cover—then you'll have introduced all these new and positive ideas to your brain. That's great! But for all of these new and positive ideas to become a part of who you are and help you be a better friend and teammate, a better classmate, a better son or daughter, and just an all around better person, then something incredibly important has to happen: The ideas need to travel those eighteen inches from your brain to your heart. And you know what's great about this? *You* have the power to make that happen. If you want these messages to travel those eighteen inches from your brain to your heart, you just need to *decide* that you want them to.

You can see messages about kindness—have them told, taught, or texted to you time and time again—but for those messages to sink in and become a part of your character, they have to travel the eighteen inches from your brain to your heart. Just eighteen inches! That's all it takes to internalize the importance of kindness. Once the journey has been made, it's up to you to take action on the message. Otherwise, the message is just words on a page.

The most important thing you can do to use your superpower, whatever it happens to be, to make a positive difference is to practice it every day. The same goes for your second superpower: kindness. The way to make kindness a part of your life is to take consistent action to be kind every day. For me, it was a matter of talking to everyone I could each day, saying something nice, and always remembering their names. For you, that might look like something else. What's important is that you focus on it and take action toward using your unique superpower and being kind every day.

So before we move on, let's ask ourselves an important question: What can I do to be kind to someone I cross paths with today?

2. Make Integrity Your Engine.

Let's think about something here: Who are you more likely to be friends with, someone you can trust or someone you know you *can't* trust? Of course, you're going to want to be friends with someone you can trust.

One thing I've learned in my twenty-plus years of running CDG Sports is that you can't have trust without integrity. What do I mean by this?

Let's imagine that you've signed up for one of my camps.

You've been excited all spring about that one week in summer where you get to come out to the field, make new friends, and have a ton of fun playing a bunch of wacky sports-based games. A few of your friends have already been to one of these camps, and they've told you that it's just the best time ever. On the first day, you show up on the field with two hundred other kids, and you're all bouncing around with excitement.

Now let's imagine something that's honestly difficult for me to even think about. What if I didn't show up? Or, what if I showed up, but I wasn't prepared? My equipment wasn't ready. All the campers had to wait while I had the coaches set everything up on all the fields. My microphone isn't working. I haven't prepared myself to speak to you about any important messages for the day.

What happened here? I asked you and all the other campers to place your trust in me that my sports camp would be fun. And I didn't show the integrity it takes to be there early, get everything ready, and show you how much it means to me that you're taking time out of your summer to be at one of my camps.

If this unbelievable thing happened, people would stop trusting me. They would stop asking me to host events. My lack of integrity would lead to the end of CDG Sports.

Okay. Whew! Let's stop thinking about that kind of thing. Instead, let's think about what integrity might look like in your life.

If you say to your friend that you're going to help them study for a test after school, but then you don't follow through because you decided to go to another friend's house to play video games, then you have proven to your friend that you can't be trusted. If you commit to raking the leaves on Saturday afternoon but then forget about it, you have proven to your parents that you are not reliable.

Integrity requires honesty, commitment, consistency, and always following through on the promises you make. It's something that, no matter what your age or background, you must commit to, internalize, and work on every day. And the way to start working on it is easy: If you say you're going to do something for someone else, then when the time comes, you do that something, no matter what.

3. Raise the Praise.

What do I mean when I say, "Raise the praise?" I mean be that person whose friends, classmates, and teammates can go to for encouragement and positivity. It's so easy in today's world to focus on the negative. Your goal should be to become that driving force for positivity.

The first step in the right direction is to recognize that it's not all about you. It's not all about your accomplishments over others. People with strong character recognize and value the hard work, accomplishments, strong qualities, and the commitment of others. Each day, take at least one opportunity to take the spotlight off of yourself and shine it on others.

When you see someone do something great, tell them. Compliment them. Point out to other people how this person did this great thing. Positivity and encouragement don't always come naturally for everyone. And these days, it often seems like it's harder than ever before to be that positive force in someone else's moment, day, or life. But the beautiful thing about positivity and encouragement is that you can *choose* to be positive and to show someone encouragement. It's all up to you. You just have to *decide* to do it. If you make that decision to be positive, let me tell you, it could make all the difference for the people around you. Raise the praise and you just might make someone's day.

4. Reshape Your Habits.

Self-discipline is usually one of those things we don't start worrying about until adulthood. But by then, it's sometimes too late. The habits we form as kids are usually the ones that are hardest to break as adults.

At a recent birthday party, dozens of kids were running around screaming, trying to get into the equipment I had brought, trying to start games before everyone was ready. Now, these were eight-year-old kids, so that kind of thing is expected. But it's important to remember that kids are never too young to learn when it's time to control themselves.

There is no "right" age to start trying to make self-discipline a key part of your character. There is also no "right" age to start thinking about the kinds of things you do each day that could be described as a habit. If your habit is to sleep in, then the longer you allow that habit to continue, the harder it will be for you to form the habit of waking up early. If you don't eat breakfast, that habit might lead to you being tired or lacking energy throughout the day. If your habit is to throw everything together at the last minute and then rush off to school or practice or another obligation, then that habit might spread to other parts of your life.

No matter how old you are, the time to start positive habits and then to build your self-discipline to stick to them is *now*. You are old enough, strong enough, and capable enough to do everything you need to do to grow as a person. As we're going to find out with all the plays in this book, it's just a matter of *deciding* to do them. Let's commit to making all the plays in this book a part of your everyday routine. Let's make them habits. And then let's show that self-discipline to keep them shining within us and shining on everyone around us!

5. Plant Your Flag.

Do your parents/guardians, teachers, coaches, friends, classmates, and teammates *really* know the kind of person you are? Do your actions and the words you use reflect your values and principles? If character is your most important piece of equipment, then it's up to you to *show* the people around you what that character looks like.

Think about this: If your friends were to describe you in one word, what would that word be? Does it match the word you would *want* them to use?

Today, starting right now, I want you to plant your flag, the one that says who you are and what you stand for. And as we go through all the Chalk Talks in this book, always remember your flag, that one word you want people to use when they describe your character, and try to live and breathe it in everything you do.

The One-Word Mindset

How would you describe yourself in one word? It's important to know the answer to this question, because that one word starts your path toward building strong character. Write that word down. Pass it that eighteen inches from your head to your heart. Internalize it.

Once you know this word, you have to live it every day. Do this, and it's how you will be remembered. It is the legacy you will leave.

Whenever I use the word *legacy*, some people tell me that kids are too young to be thinking about things like that. But here's what I think: When you're a kid, that's the perfect time to start thinking about your legacy. We're all so quick to ask young people what they want to be when they grow up, when the more important question is, "What do you want to be *right now*?"

Without the answer to that question, it's not possible to make character your best piece of equipment.

What do you want to be remembered for? For me, it would be nice to know that people remember the quality of my camps or the fun they had at the birthday parties or the things they learned at the talks I give. But more than that, I want to be remembered for the impact I have on the people I meet each day. I want to be remembered for making people feel good about themselves. For caring. For treating everyone equally and with respect. For remembering *them*.

In the end, being known for something positive, building a reputation for strong character, leaving a legacy—it isn't about you. It's not about your accomplishments. It's about the way you make others feel.

Once you know your one-word mindset, do everything you can to live it every day. Be who you want to be. Build others up. Make them know that they are significant. Give them all you've got. Whatever you do, don't just do it for yourself. Think about how it will affect others. Focus on making a difference, and not just on success, and you will be remembered for more than just the things you do. You'll be remembered for *who you are*.

INSTANT REPLAY

1. FIND YOUR SUPERPOWER

2. MAKE INTEGRITY YOUR ENGINE

3. RAISE THE PRAISE

4. RESHAPE YOUR HABITS

5. PLANT YOUR FLAG

CHALK TALK #2

Five Plays to Define Your Character

A lot of people say, "You need to be more confident."
I say, "Just be you."
—Serena Williams

My mom was one of thirteen kids in her family. Thirteen! Can you imagine having twelve brothers and sisters? That whole huge family lived on a small farm near a mountain town in Puerto Rico. They didn't have a lot of money or a lot of space, but there was always opportunity to stay home and try to make a life in those conditions.

At the age of seventeen, Mom made the choice to break out of her comfort zone and travel to Pittsburgh, PA, in the hopes of working and earning enough money to send back to her family so that everyone's lives could improve, little by little.

Between her young age, her lack of experience, and the fact that she didn't speak English all that well, my mother was fortunate to find a job, first as a nanny and cook and later as a cafeteria worker at a children's hospital.

Talk about discipline and consistency! Every day, seven days a week, for thirty-five years of her life, she would get to the hospital at five-thirty in the morning and work the same shift.

She did all of this without speaking much English at first. She taught herself along the way and now speaks fluently.

After I was born, she had no choice but to allow other people to help raise me. She didn't make enough money for childcare, and my father had challenges with alcohol that made it difficult to trust him to care for me while my mom was at work. These were challenging times, but Mom stayed the course. She worked hard every day to put food on the table. Whatever struggles she faced, she relied on her character as her best piece of equipment.

What my mom's story taught me is that you will be known more for your character than you will for your accomplishments. This is why it's so important to start building strong character now, long before people start calling you an adult. If it happens when you're young, it's easier to internalize it, easier to take it that eighteen inches from your head to your heart. It becomes a more consistent and natural part of you.

So, how do we *define* our character? Here's the playbook:

1. Choose to Have Strong Character

Wait a minute! Can we just *choose* to have strong character? Well, yes. In fact, as we've talked about a couple of times already in this book, *choosing* to do something is the first step to making any positive change in your life.

If you want to be a better hockey player, you have to *choose* to commit to practicing harder and more often. If you want to be a better student, you have to *choose* to spend more time on studying and learning. The actions that follow (whether it's getting up at 6:00 a.m. every day to put in the extra ice time or spending an extra hour each night reviewing the day's lessons at school) are what will make your hope a reality. But step one is always that you have to truly and genuinely *choose* that this is what you want. It's that eighteen inches principle again. All the wisdom in the world doesn't matter if we don't choose to make it a part of who we are and how we define ourselves.

Today, before you finish this Chalk Talk, what I would like for you to say to yourself is this: "I've decided to be a self-supporting person." What does that mean? Well, when you look at the word *support*, what do you think of? To me, I think of how I might support someone else by being encouraging and enthusiastic about what they are doing and helping them in any way I can. If you're going to decide to be a self-supporting person, then that means doing those same things for yourself.

It means choosing to be a positive person. It means being positive in the ways you think about and talk about yourself. It means expressing positive body language. It means choosing to be happy and supportive of others.

All of these changes might seem challenging at first, but don't worry. I'm not asking you to make all of these changes all at once. Growing as a person, showing that great character every day, will take some time, some patience, and plenty of commitment. But I know two things for sure: First, the most important step is to *choose* to make these changes and to grow as a person; and second, if you commit yourself to this choice, you *will* succeed!

2. Be a Builder, Not a Bulldozer

When you hear the word *builder*, what do you think of? Probably someone who works to construct things. If you're like me, you think about someone building a house. They're using the materials they have available to them and creating something better.

Now, what do you think when you hear the word *bulldozer*? I think about a giant machine knocking things down. Where a builder is building something better, a bulldozer is taking something and destroying it.

If we're talking about construction, both a builder and a bulldozer have their uses. But when we're talking about how we interact with other people . . .

"All right!" I called out cheerfully to a class of seventh graders. "Who's ready for some team-building activities?"

No one spoke up.

"C'mon," I said, "I know there must be someone here who's ready to have some fun!"

An uncomfortable couple of seconds passed, and still, no one spoke up. Everyone just sat there looking at me uneasily as I smiled back at them.

Finally, someone stepped forward. "Yeah, let's do this!" she said. Her name was Rachel, and I'll never forget that name because she completely saved the day. She helped me not just by breaking the silence, but by leading one of the two stations I had set up for the first activity. Before she spoke up, there just wasn't any energy in the room at all. When she broke the silence, she energized everyone. When she volunteered to help me, she demonstrated to everyone else that it was okay to participate.

I was standing there in front of an unenthusiastic audience, and Rachel chose to *build me up*.

It's almost never a good thing to say that there are certain "kinds" of people in this world. But you know what? There's one case where I think it's absolutely true: There are two kinds of people in life—those who build others up, and those who try to break them down. It helps me to think of the first group as *builders* and the second group as *bulldozers*.

In this moment, Rachel was being a builder. The impact she had on me was infectious. Her positivity stirred me into saying something positive too. I was so grateful and so happy about her leadership that I said during one of the activities, "You know what, Rachel? You should run for class president. You're an amazing leader."

At the time, I didn't think about what saying this might mean to Rachel. It didn't occur to me that, right there, I had chosen to be a builder, as well. But after the exercises were over and everyone had left for their afternoon classes, Rachel came up to me, gave me a high-five, and said something I wasn't expecting. "So, Coach Dave, I just wanted to let you know that I've thought about it, and I *am* going to run for class president."

For a moment, I just stood there in amazement. I was like, *Wow!* Not because it surprised me that Rachel had recognized how perfect she was for the role, but because it was a great example of something you and I talked about in Chalk Talk #1. It was that important second superpower we all have. That superpower is our ability to say something kind, something positive, something that has the potential to change not just the way a person is feeling about their day, but the way a person thinks about themselves.

"Listen," I said once I got over my initial excitement, "you just made my day by telling me that. And I just want you to know that I wish you the best and encourage you to follow your heart."

This was one of the most memorable moments I've had in my time as a youth coach. If you take the opportunity to say something encouraging to someone—to build them up—you may not even realize the impact you're having on that person. They might just smile and move on with their day (and even then, you've done something incredibly positive by having the courage to boost someone up), but every once in a while, what you say could change how a person thinks about themselves. Even without meaning to, you could have a positive impact on a person's life.

So if you're thinking something kind about someone, say it out loud. Be a builder. Take every opportunity to build up someone's self-esteem and confidence. If you think about it, and if you work at it, then you'll soon realize how being a builder is every bit as easy as being a bulldozer, the kind of person who says mean things and breaks others down.

Whatever you do and whoever you're with, let's commit to being a builder and not a bulldozer. Make the decision—send this idea that eighteen inches from your brain to your heart—to be positive, build up the people you're with, and leave them feeling a little bit better than when you started.

Speaking of which, here's an everyday action that you can practice and turn into one of those positive habits we're trying to form. Yes, it's true that first impressions are often the most important, but what about the *last* impression you leave with someone? As I'm thinking about how to be a builder, I make it a point to always end any conversation with another person with a compliment or a positive remark—something that will let them know I care about them, I enjoyed talking to them, and I'm looking forward to seeing them again soon.

Think about all the different people you cross paths with every day. Think of the difference you could make if you said something positive to each one of those people, something that would make them feel better about themselves and good about the kind of person you are! So, whether it's the first thing you say or the last thing you say, each time you meet up with someone, think of it as a new opportunity to build them up.

3. Recognize the Power of Kindness

Once, while reading through social media, I learned about a charity started by a local ten-year-old named Emma. This amazing fifth grader had been inspired by a story about how one of the biggest and most often overlooked challenges that many homeless people face is related to their socks. It seems like such a small thing—something few of us ever think about—the importance of warm, clean, comfortable socks. But when you're homeless, and you're living outdoors in cold weather, not having good socks can be a huge problem.

When Emma learned about this, she decided to do more than just think about a kindness that could make a huge difference. She took *action* to spread that kindness. She started a charity to collect donations of new socks that she would then donate to local organizations helping the homeless.

Her kindness inspired me so much that I changed CDG Sports' annual holiday ice skating event to help benefit Emma's charity and further spread the kindness she showed. Now, every year, the day after Christmas, CDG Sports sponsors an ice skating event where the cost to get into the rink to skate is a donation of one new pair of socks for Emma's charity. At each event, we have collected hundreds of pairs of socks, and we're only one small example of what Emma's kindness has inspired. Her charity collects thousands and thousands of socks every year.

There are three things that I have learned about spreading

acts of kindness. First, you're going to be amazed by how far your kindness reaches, even if the act is a small one. Second, you're *always* going to feel good about yourself for choosing to spread kindness. And third? When you feel good about yourself, you start thinking about yourself and talking to yourself in more positive ways, which helps improve your habits, and in turn, builds strong character.

As you're thinking about actions you can take to make kindness a habit that travels eighteen inches from your brain to your heart, just remember that *every* kindness, no matter how big or small, counts. You don't have to start a big charity organization. Every kind word, small gesture, little gift, or minor act of thoughtfulness will spread. Even small kindnesses can make a huge impact—not just for the people you give them to, but for the people they then interact with during their day, and also, for yourself.

4. Sometimes, You Just Have to Show Up

It was raining last night. It was chilly, foggy, and miserable outside. After an exhausting day, I wanted nothing more than to just curl up on my couch and rest. But I had somewhere to be. A mother of two middle-school-age boys who had been through a few of my camps had invited me to come watch her two sons play in an all-star hockey game at a nearby skating rink. She'd said that it would mean so much to them if I showed up to watch. I'd committed to this a week prior, but I'll be honest; the rink was outdoors, and one look at the weather had me wanting to call and cancel.

But then I thought, *You know what? That's the easy way out.*

It would have been so easy to make an excuse. Something

had come up at work. I wasn't feeling well. I'd forgotten about a commitment I'd made at home. But calling up and canceling would not have been consistent with who I always try to be.

So I went to the game. Despite the weather, the place was packed. There were so many people that I couldn't find the parents who'd invited me. When it was over, I headed home thinking that the parents wouldn't have even noticed I'd come.

The next day, a text message came in from the mom. "Hey, Coach Dave. I saw you at the game yesterday and didn't get a chance to say hi, but I wanted to thank you for being there. It meant so much to my boys to know that you were there to support them."

There are a few lessons I took from this story. First, it's just another example of how a little kindness and positivity can spread and make everything better. The positivity of this text carried me through that whole day.

Second, sometimes, showing kindness and positivity is just a matter of *showing up*, even if you don't want to. Being there for someone else is the absolute best way to show them you care and that you support them.

Last but definitely not least, this story reminds me that it's not enough to show strong character just some of the time. If you're positive one minute, and negative the next, you change the impression people have of you. If you're spreading kindness one day, it all comes undone if you're mean to someone the next.

Strong character requires you to always do what you say you will. Always show up. Always be kind. Always seek opportunities to build up others. Do this, and people will come to know you as someone they value and want to be around.

5. Let Determination Be Your Guide

"Ready, Set, Run!" is a 5K training program for kids of all ages and skill levels—from competitive runners to couch potatoes, we train together to run a 5K. Each week, we train for the run, but we also have a character lesson. At the end of the practice, we sit down and discuss the magical effects of empathy or how important it is to be consistent.

At the end of our twelve weeks together, we set up that final 5K run. We invite parents and other family members and loved ones to come run with us. The only requirement for joining the run is that you have to try to do what ultramarathon runner Dean Karnazes once said: "Run when you can, walk when you have to, crawl if you must; just never give up."

We didn't expect everyone to run the full 5K without stopping. That wasn't the point. The point was to be a better person at the end of the program than we were when we started. Whatever it took to complete the 5K, as long as we completed it, that would be a success.

Everyone lined up at the start of the race. I stepped out with my cap gun and my stopwatch. And over the speaker system, I announced, "On your marks, get set, go!"

By the end of the run, some of the kids had beaten their personal best. Others completed a 5K for the first time in their lives. Some had to do more walking than running. But that's not what I'll remember about this one particular run. Yes, everyone who ran showed the determination to finish—and that's fantastic! Just as importantly, though, all the kids and parents who finished the run stuck around to cheer for the ones who hadn't yet crossed the finish line. Some had finished the run in just twenty minutes, and an hour later, they were still cheering on the kids who hadn't made it yet.

None of them had to be told to do this. They showed their strong character by sticking around and building up their fellow runners. Whatever it took, and however long it took, they stayed and cheered until the last runner crossed the line.

It was so hot that afternoon. By the time the last runner got to the final lap, sweat was pouring down his cheeks. Hundreds of runners were lining both sides of the track. This last runner had to walk for most of the final lap, but by the time he came around to that home stretch and heard the crowd, he broke into a run. The closer he came to the finish line, the louder the crowd cheered, and the faster he ran.

A huge cheer went up when the runner ripped off his shirt and started swinging it over his head as he crossed the finish line. It was one of the proudest moments I've ever had as a coach. I was proud that the last runner showed so much determination to finish the race, but I couldn't have been prouder of the support and kindness the other kids showed by sticking around to help *everyone* cross the finish line. That's the power of spreading kindness, of being a builder, and demonstrating strong character.

———

The final message of this Chalk Talk is this: It takes hard work to make change. Showing strong character means working on yourself as hard as you would at soccer practice, or when you're studying for a test at school. It requires consistent and persistent dedication.

Working on yourself means practicing positive daily habits. For most people, that means exercising, reading, learning new things, following through on your promises, meeting (and exceeding) the expectations you set for yourself and that others set for you, and focusing on doing something nice for yourself and for others every day.

It's not easy to make all of these things a part of your daily life, but think about it this way: What's more important than getting better as a person each day? The work is hard, but the reward makes it worth it. I know you can do this!

INSTANT REPLAY

1. CHOOSE TO HAVE STRONG CHARACTER

2. BE A BUILDER, NOT A BULLDOZER

3. RECOGNIZE THE POWER OF KINDNESS

4. SOMETIMES YOU JUST HAVE TO SHOW UP

5. LET DETERMINATION BE YOUR GUIDE

CHALK TALK #3

Five Plays to Make Empathy Your Next Superpower

Empathy is understanding the struggle of the person across from you. When you bring that to your team, you become much more than just an athlete. You become someone everyone can count on.

–Abby Wambach

In the first two Chalk Talks, we thought about our superpowers. Your first superpower is completely unique to you. For me, it's always remembering people's names. For you, it might look a little different. Maybe your superpower is that you're a great storyteller, or maybe you're an excellent athlete or artist, or maybe you're good at math or making people laugh. The only thing I can tell you for sure about your first superpower is that it's a positive trait, and the best way for you to grow as a person is to accept that superpower, make it an important part of your character, and work on it every day.

Your second superpower, as we've been talking about, is kindness. Everybody possesses the power of kindness. It's just a matter of *choosing* to be kind. It's about being a builder and not a bulldozer, and about taking action to spread kindness in every situation and to everyone you meet.

Here in Chalk Talk #3, we're going to discuss your third superpower, and it's one that's so important, it gets a Chalk Talk all to itself: empathy.

Okay, so what is empathy? The best way I can describe it is that it's the ability to put yourself in someone else's shoes and truly understand how that person feels.

But that's just a *description* of the word. A definition. The best way, I think, to relate to you what empathy really means is to *show* you, and the best way I know how to do that is through a story.

I wasn't always as outgoing and enthusiastic as I am these days. There have been periods of my life when things were a little darker for me, and one of those periods was my junior year of high school. Back then, I was having a little trouble at home. My self-confidence was down. I had turned inward, closed myself off to others, and my body language and expressions were all just so negative.

The worst part about it? I didn't even notice. I was so stuck in my own head that I didn't realize how I was projecting so much negativity onto the people around me.

My world cultures teacher, Mrs. Peel, was the first person to notice that my light was a little dimmer lately. "Dave," she said to me one day after class, "would you like to come into school early tomorrow and have breakfast with me?"

This invitation took me by surprise because Mrs. Peel was one of the best teachers at my high school, and I couldn't imagine why she would want to spend any of her free time with someone like me. Even though I was in a negative place at the time, I thought it was cool that she would ask me to join her.

The next morning at breakfast, we sat across from each other in the cafeteria, and Mrs. Peel asked questions and listened. That's it. She didn't have any kind of special wisdom to give me. She just asked questions and listened.

And you know what? It made all the difference. A kind, caring adult was giving me the chance to just talk about what was going on in my life, and because she listened, showed her concern, and helped me see my good qualities, that one meeting helped me understand that things could be better for me. After that day, my mood, my mindset, my self-esteem, the enthusiasm I brought with me to school—everything improved.

It all started because Mrs. Peel noticed my body language, the way I was acting around others, and the words I was using. Because she noticed these things that not even I was noticing, and because she was able to put herself in my shoes and relate to my struggles, she helped me see myself in a new light and then start spreading that light to others. I'll never forget it.

This is the best example of the power of empathy I've ever been a part of. There is unbelievable power in being able to see and understand what someone else might be going through. Empathy is what helps us to recognize that the things a person says or does—or the way they say or do them—might not reflect exactly what's in their heart. Maybe they're going through a difficult time in their lives, just like I was back in high school. Maybe they just heard some sad news that has put them in a bad mood. Maybe they're just having a tough day. You won't know unless you genuinely listen, ask questions, focus on the positive in them, and try to put yourself in their shoes.

You've heard that expression, I'm sure: "You have to put yourself in the other person's shoes." What it means is that we shouldn't judge someone too quickly. It means that we can't completely understand who they are, why they're behaving like they are, or how they're feeling until we truly imagine ourselves in their place—until we *empathize* with them.

We all wear different shoes. Our friends might have similar shoes. Some of the kids we know from class or on the playground might have similar shoes. Some of the kids we've never met might have similar shoes. And there are many, many more—both friends and strangers—who wear different shoes than we do. Many of us don't even wear the same shoes two days in a row. We have different shoes for different days and different activities.

Something very similar is true about the people around us. We might be similar in some ways. Maybe we have the same opinions, or like the same things. Maybe we have similar smiles or similar hobbies. But no matter what we look like, and no matter what we like and dislike, we all have different points of view. We will agree on some things and disagree on others. What's common to the other person, what's fun to them, how they like to spend their time, may not be the same for you. But that's okay.

The next time you're in school or on the playground or at the park, look at the other kids' shoes. Now, when you look, don't think about their shoes as a way to judge them. Just like you can't assume that the beat-up old shoes belong to someone without the means to buy new ones, you can't use another person's shoes to judge who they are, deep down. You can't use shoes as a measure of a person's character. Instead, when you look at those shoes, think about the perspective of the person who's wearing them. How would *you* feel if you were that person?

The next time you see someone being picked on, or teased, or who's sitting alone at lunch, put yourself in that person's shoes. Imagine how you would feel to be standing or sitting where they are. I mean it—*really* ask yourself, "How would I feel?"

Don't worry if it's hard for you to do this at first. Showing true empathy doesn't come easily to most people. The effort, though, is worth it, because empathy is one of the most important superpowers you can have as someone who is trying to connect with the people around you.

Empathy is important because, on the simplest level, it makes you a more caring person. It makes you a better friend, classmate, teammate, and son or daughter. If we dig deeper, though, we see that having this ability to identify and accept the way other people think and feel will help us feel better about *ourselves*. If you treat people kindly, you're going to feel good about yourself. It's the most natural thing in the world! On top of that, by showing empathy, you become well-liked by others. It's an amazing thing that happens; the energy you put out usually has a way of coming back to you. Treat others with empathy, and they will be more likely to treat you the same way.

To me, *empathy* is actually a verb. Just like brushing your teeth or doing your homework, it needs to be practiced regularly as a part of your daily routine. This is the only way to guide it that eighteen inches from your head to your heart.

So, how do we take empathy from an idea or a feeling and make it into our third superpower? Here's the playbook:

1. Listen from the Heart

"Knock, knock."

"Who's there?"

"Interrupting cow."

"Interrupting c—"

"Moo!"

I like to tell this joke whenever I'm talking to a group about how important it is to listen first without interrupting.

Isn't that annoying when someone isn't listening? Or they interrupt with their thoughts before you're finished speaking?

The superpower of empathy is all about understanding how the other person feels, and how can we fully understand the other person if we don't really *listen*?

You know what I've noticed about kids playing on the playground? First, they will sometimes argue. More importantly, when kids argue, most of the time, the reason they're arguing is because someone just isn't listening. They argue because there's a misunderstanding. Almost every argument could be avoided if both people involved took a minute to actually listen to and understand the other person.

This doesn't just happen on the playground either. Sometimes, even I don't listen quite as well as I should. It's a challenging skill to learn and use every day. But the more you practice, the easier it becomes. Once you start listening to other people's points of view, and truly trying to understand where they're coming from, you'll find it so much easier to understand and empathize with how they're feeling.

Listening from the heart is about so much more than just preventing arguments and misunderstandings too. If you really listen, you'll be amazed at how much you can learn about the people around you. People often ask me what my secret is for remembering everyone's names and a few things about their lives. Even if I haven't seen them in a few months, I'll go up and ask them about how they enjoyed that trip they were telling me about last time. They are always amazed that I remembered something so specific about them.

But there's really no big secret here. All you have to do is listen, and you have to listen from the heart. What does this mean? First, it means that you can't just be in a conversation waiting for your turn to talk. If we're going to understand where someone is coming from, what they're feeling, and how they're thinking, then it requires us to *hear* what they're saying, *process* what they mean, and *empathize* with how they're feeling when they say what they're saying.

If that sounds difficult, then it might help to practice something called *active listening*. There's a game I like to play to help get everyone's enthusiasm going at the start of a school assembly.

"Okay," I'll call out to the crowd. "We're going to count to ten, and we're going to do it as a group. But there's a catch! Only one person can say a number at a time. If two people speak up and say a number at the same time, then we have to start all over at one. Do you think you can get to ten?"

Every group always thinks they can do it. It sounds easy, right? But then, every time when I say go, three or four people will yell out "one" at the same time. Everyone laughs and now they see that this isn't going to be so easy.

So they'll start over and do a little better next time. Maybe they make it to four before two people speak up at once. Then we go through it again and again, letting them see how the mistakes are happening.

Recently, I had a group make it all the way up to ten. It took them six or seven tries, and in the second-to-last attempt, they made it all the way to nine before two people chimed in and everyone started laughing with frustration. With that group, I couldn't have been more impressed by their determination. But what was more impressive was how they mastered the point of the game: If you want to work well as a group (or as a friend), you have to *listen first*.

The next time you're having a conversation with someone, think about that as your goal. Listen first. Listen from the heart. Do everything you can to really hear and understand what the other person is saying. Then, when you feel like you have a better understanding of what they're thinking, saying, and feeling, try out the next play . . .

2. Ask Meaningful Questions

This is going to sound funny, but you want to know the best way to show the other person that you're really listening? Ask them questions! People enjoy answering questions, especially if those questions show them that you're trying hard to empathize with them and understand where they're coming from.

What does that look like? Well, let's imagine that you and I are having a conversation about a trip I recently took to Puerto Rico, where my family is from. Some meaningful questions you might ask could be:

"Did you stay in a hotel or with family and friends?"

"How long was the trip?"

"What cities did you visit?"

"Did you spend any time at the beach?"

"Did you go to any baseball games?"

Asking these kinds of questions not only shows the other person that you care about them; it helps you better understand them as well, which is what empathy is all about.

3. Avoid the Assumption Obstacle

Making assumptions about people, and about the meaning behind what they're saying or doing, is almost first nature for most people. It's what causes us to make judgments about people based on their appearance without first asking questions and getting to know them.

The thing about assumptions, though, is that they are far too often wrong. You remember that counting game I like to play with the crowds at my assemblies? Well, there's another game I like to play right after we're done with that one, and it always gets a big reaction. Without explaining what I'm doing, I'll go into my bag of props and pick out a can of food and a spoon. First, I show the can to everyone in the audience, making sure they see that the can is labeled *Dog Food*. Then, without saying anything, I'll open the can, dig in with my spoon, and start eating.

Every time, most of the audience will start groaning and hollering about how gross it is to eat dog food. That's when I smile and go back to my bag to show them another can wrapped in a *Hormel Chili* label. I explain to them that before the assembly, I switched the labels. What looks like a can of dog food is actually just a good old-fashioned can of chili.

The message is simple: You can't judge something or someone based just on assumptions. But if you take a moment to listen from the heart, and if you ask the right questions, you'll quickly learn the truth.

4. Be There in Body and Mind

For many people—and I'm very much including myself in this—the first instinct is to talk about ourselves and what we're doing. We'll fill the conversation with our plans, our likes and dislikes, our opinions and ideas. But if we're practicing empathy, then we have to recognize that, usually, what the other person is more interested in talking about is themselves.

Being present for others is all about giving them the chance to speak, offering your undivided attention, listening from the heart, and this is a big one, using your body language to show them that you are here, you care, and you are interested in what they have to say.

Body language is a difficult thing to manage for most people. Unless you're thinking about it and working on it, it's just so easy to accidentally show the other person that you're not completely listening or empathizing with them. You might be leaning away, making a funny face, or looking around the room.

Step one for managing your body language to help show your empathy is to make eye contact. Look at the other person while they are talking to you, and it will go such a long way to showing them how much you care. I know that this can be challenging for some people. I have a hard time looking people in the eyes all the time too. If you have trouble with this, the best trick is to look at the bridge of their nose or that space between their eyebrows. To them, it will look just like eye contact.

In any conversation or interaction with another person, always remember that your *presence* is your greatest *present*. Show them—in both body and mind—that you are here and that you care, and not only will they respond to you in a more positive way, but you will be stunned by how much more you learn about them, and how much stronger your empathy superpower will be as a result.

5. Think Outside Yourself

For almost everyone, we spend most of our time thinking about our own ideas, challenges, and successes. With our final play, we're going to think about how important it is to make room in your thoughts and in your life for what other people are doing, how they're feeling, and what might be meaningful to them.

As a daily practice, let's spend some time thinking about the other people in our lives. Think about what is meaningful to them at this moment—what they're going through, what they might be struggling with, what they might be proud of or happy about right now, what they might need to make their day a little brighter. It only takes a few minutes each day to do this. If it helps, you can even make a list of the people you need to think about and then sit down and work through the list each day. The more you do this, the more natural it will become, and the easier this play will be to run in your everyday life. If you spend time each day taking the focus off of yourself and thinking about others, it becomes one of those habits that travels eighteen inches from your brain to your heart.

Okay, next, let's think about meeting someone new. Whenever we meet someone new, it's usually much easier to think about what we *don't* like about them. Our differences are just so much clearer at first than our similarities. Believe it or not, we do this even with the people who eventually become our closest friends.

But if we try hard enough to get to know them, we discover that *everyone* has at least one quality we can relate to. If you're an athlete and the person you meet doesn't like sports at all, that doesn't mean they don't have any good qualities in common with you. Maybe you both like the same music or the same show. Maybe you're both really good at science. Maybe you both collect Pokémon cards. If you ask, maybe you'll find out that they live in the same neighborhood as you, or they go to the same place as you for vacation every summer.

And we haven't even gotten into their personality yet! Maybe they're very enthusiastic. Maybe they're really organized or purposeful. Maybe they're funny or even just quick to laugh. Maybe they're incredibly kind and thoughtful.

In my life, of course I've encountered people who don't wind up being my friend. But I have yet to meet anyone who doesn't have good qualities to admire and appreciate. If you make it a habit to look for those good qualities in the people around you—at school, in your neighborhood, in your sports or after school activities—empathy will come more naturally.

———

Learning empathy is such a big part of growing as a person, and it's also one of the most difficult skills to make a part of our lives and how we think about other people.

So, as a final message and maybe a little bit of a challenge, I'm going to ask one more thing of you today: Try something totally new. Something you have never done before. Something you never thought you would have enjoyed. Bonus points if it's something that a person you don't completely relate to enjoys doing. This is true at every point of your life, but while you're young, it's especially important: Try out different experiences, activities, and ways of looking at things. Get outside your comfort zone a little. The more you do this, the easier it will be for you to understand *why* people do the things they do, think the way they think, or act the way they act. Experience is the quickest path to empathy.

INSTANT REPLAY

1. LISTEN FROM THE HEART

2. ASK MEANINGFUL QUESTIONS

3. AVOID THE ASSUMPTION OBSTACLE

4. BE THERE IN BODY AND MIND

5. THINK OUTSIDE YOURSELF

CHALK TALK #4

Five Plays for Creating a Positive Mindset

Every strike brings me closer to the next home run.
–Babe Ruth

---

n seventh grade, I had a gym teacher named Mr. Wyland. He was the kind of person I wanted to model myself after—one of those people you just love having as a coach. He was just an awesome guy.

During one of our gym class units, we learned about the sport of wrestling. Having grown up in foster homes the first seven years of my life, I lacked confidence during my elementary school years, and that was especially true in seventh grade. I didn't know much about wrestling, except that, truthfully, I didn't really *enjoy* it. But one day during gym class, Mr. Wyland pulled me aside and said, "You know what, Dave? I see you working hard out there, and I think you might have what it takes to be really good at this sport."

Mr. Wyland's encouragement was all I needed to commit to learning how to be a wrestler. It turned out that my new elementary school would have a special assembly once a year, where all the students in every grade level would come down to the gym to watch everyone on the wrestling team compete in a tournament. At first, I didn't think too much about it, but then when the day came and I saw all those people watching us from the stands, I just completely froze up. The nerves, the intimidation, the fear that I'd make a mistake—it all got the better of me. My opponent pinned me in about three seconds.

After it was over, I was so upset and embarrassed that it was all I could do to get back to the sidelines and sit down so I could hang my head in shame. There were other opportunities for me to wrestle after that, but I passed on all of them, not wanting to get humiliated again.

After the tournament, I shuffled back to the locker room and gathered my stuff as quickly as I could and left without saying anything to any of my teammates or Mr. Wyland. That weekend was pretty miserable. For me, the biggest thing wasn't that I'd fallen apart in front of my classmates and teammates; it was that it felt like I'd let Mr. Wyland down.

Just before my first gym class the next week, Mr. Wyland pulled me aside, saying he wanted to talk to me about something. My heart started racing because I had a feeling it would be about the tournament, and he would want to tell me about all these things I'd done wrong.

"Dave," he said as he put his hand on my shoulder, "I just want you to know how proud I am of you."

My heart stopped racing. Confused, I looked up at him with big eyes.

"I mean it," he said. "I'm proud of you because you took the risk of joining the team even though you had no experience in wrestling. You came to practice every day and worked hard. Everything you learned, you showed a passion for it. Now, I know you got pinned in the tournament, but that's not how to measure yourself. How you measure yourself is about whether you showed up to practice every day, whether you tried hard, and whether you improved. And you did that every day, Dave. I'm proud of you, and you should be proud too. You have no reason to feel embarrassed about what happened in that tournament."

Mr. Wyland taught me so many things in that moment. First, let's think about how he demonstrated the *empathy* to recognize that one of his wrestlers was embarrassed about how he'd performed in front of his classmates. And even after a weekend had passed, he pulled me aside and took the time to show that he understood, that he cared, and that he believed there was no reason for me to be embarrassed. In fact, he said I should be *proud*. His empathy immediately changed the way I felt about what happened. That's a lesson for all of us, one we can use any time we see someone who is struggling or feeling down about themselves.

We already know that empathy is one of the greatest superpowers you can have. What I'd like to focus on for this Chalk Talk is how Mr. Wyland's words highlighted a different and more positive way of thinking about *yourself*, your performance, and how to stay true to who you are and what you believe in. When he pulled me aside that day, Mr. Wyland gave me the foundation for a new way of thinking—a positive *mindset* that would keep me focused on what was most important during my elementary years and beyond. This mindset has kept me growing as a person for all these years since.

How can we develop the kind of positive mindset that Mr. Wyland taught me back when I was in elementary school? Here's the playbook:

1. Build an Unwavering Belief in Yourself

Let's start with a little exercise. How do you talk to yourself? When you think about yourself and your own qualities, do your thoughts sound more positive or negative? Do you treat yourself like a builder or a bulldozer with the words you use in your head or when you're alone?

After my embarrassing performance at the wrestling tournament, I spent a weekend tearing myself down. My thoughts and feelings about myself were not at all positive. And that definitely wasn't the only time during my middle school years that this happened.

Maybe there have been times in your life when you got down on yourself, and you noticed that no matter what you tried, your thoughts were all so negative. It doesn't matter how old you are, where you come from, or how positive your thoughts tend to be; when something negative happens to you, it's very easy to fall into the trap of becoming your own worst *bulldozer*.

This is why, as the first play to build a positive mindset, we need to work on how to keep the *belief in our potential* running high, even throughout the tougher times.

It starts with remembering that there will always be setbacks in life. No one is perfect, right? When it feels as if we have let ourselves down, let our friends or teammates down, let our coaches or teachers or parents down—and believe me, I've been there too!—it's usually a good idea to spend some time reminding ourselves about our best qualities.

You know what I do whenever I'm feeling down? I make a list of all the things I like about myself. The fancy term for this kind of thing is *positive affirmation*. When I make my list of positive affirmations, I usually include things like, "I'm a really good listener," or "My laugh makes people smile," or "People like the way I tell stories."

Your list might have some of those same things on it, or they might be very different from mine. Whatever you write down, try to focus on the qualities of your character, the personal qualities that make you the kind of person who people at home, at school, on your teams, and in your community enjoy being around. Maybe these are qualities that you share with others every day, and maybe there are some things you can do to show the people in your life these good qualities more often. Either way, these qualities are positive, and they are true to who you are.

Okay, so now you have a list of your best qualities. Next, let's start adding some of the positive *actions* you can take every day to help develop the great person you are. "I'm a good teammate on my baseball team," or "I always study hard for my tests," or "I do my part to clean up the house every day."

Finally, it's a great idea to add some of your favorite abilities to the list. "I'm the best ball handler on the basketball team," or "I'm really good at math," or "I'm a thoughtful friend."

The more qualities, actions, and abilities you write down, the better you will start to feel about yourself in the moment. The more you return to the list, the more these positive observations will become a part of the way you talk to yourself, even if you're experiencing a challenging time.

You know what I like to do with my list? I repeat it to myself every day. I usually think about my list in the morning before work, and sometimes I think about it at the end of the day—especially if I've had a tough day, which is something that happens to all of us! Thinking about your list can happen at any point in the day that works for you. Right in the middle of the day? That's totally fine. Whenever things get difficult, or you notice negative thoughts about yourself, or you just need to build yourself up to meet a challenge, returning to that list is always a great idea that will help you feel better about yourself and readier to face whatever is ahead of you.

It might sound simple, but having this list and returning to it every day can make all the difference in how you "talk" to yourself. And this is incredibly important, because how you "talk" to yourself goes a long way toward defining who you are. If you concentrate on saying and thinking positive things about yourself, then you start to develop an unwavering belief in yourself. Do this often enough, and in time, that positivity will travel eighteen inches from your head to your heart, and you will be a more confident, positive person with a positive mindset.

2. Spread Your Enthusiasm

This past summer at one of my sports camps, I had the pleasure of meeting a fifth grader named Matthew. He had just moved into the school district a few weeks before camp started. In fact, he'd moved to our area from three whole states away. Here was a kid who didn't know anything about his new hometown, let alone have any friends. What was so special about Matthew was that he didn't let this get to him.

The first thing I noticed about Matthew was his infectious smile. He was always shining his big smile on everyone, and it seemed to have the power to make everyone else smile back at him. The next thing I noticed were the large corrective glasses he wore. They reminded me of the ones I used to wear as a kid. But the most important thing I noticed about Matthew was that, even though this was a sports camp, and even though he wasn't the best athlete, the other campers all wanted to be on his team. Everyone was naturally drawn to him. He made friends easily, and he did it all with his positive attitude and enthusiasm. There was just something magnetic about him.

But how did he do this? It started every morning the second his mom dropped him off. He would come out of the car saying, "Hey, Coach Dave! You'll never guess what happened to me this morning." Then he would launch into a story that would have me smiling all the way through.

We have theme days every day of sports camp. One day will be team spirit day. Another will be funny hat day. Another is mohawk and mustaches day. Every day, Matthew went all out. He wore a full baseball uniform. He had the funniest hat. He wore a motorcycle T-shirt and a fake mustache. He was just hilarious in his own special way. And he carried this level of enthusiasm with him wherever he went and in whatever he did. The score never mattered. If he struck out, he'd come away clapping, "Okay, let's go!" and cheering on the next player up.

It's an amazing ability, being able to make the people around you feel special. It's what I call making everyone you meet feel like an MVP (which you'll remember stands for Most Valuable *Person*). This is exactly the kind of thing Matthew did for everyone at camp, and it's exactly what all of us could do a little more of every day as we work on building our positive mindset.

"But hold on, Coach Dave," you might be saying. "How can I make *everyone* feel like the Most Valuable Person?"

It all starts with enthusiasm. Of course, enthusiasm comes more naturally for some people than others. Just like Matthew, for as long as I can remember, I've had enthusiasm just shooting out of my ears every day! But that's not the case for many other people. Fortunately, there are ways to make our enthusiasm shine even if we're not always feeling up for it, and even if it doesn't come as naturally.

It starts by recognizing that the "Big Time," (as Coach Frosty Westering calls it in one of my all-time favorite books, *Make the Big Time Where You Are*), can happen *anywhere*—even in the kinds of places where we might not normally think about it. For example, a few days ago, I was visiting a home improvement store when I heard someone call out my name. I turned and saw a young girl and her dad waving to me. It took me a second to recognize her from one of my summer camps, but then it came to me. Her name was Hannah.

Now, it would have been the easiest thing in the world for me to smile, wave back, and just keep shopping. But being enthusiastic—making everyone you communicate with feel like the Most Valuable Person—calls for you to take that extra step. I went over to them, shook Dad's hand, and said to Hannah, "Hey, it's great to see you, Hannah! What's new?"

By going over to them, it showed that I wanted to make time for them, which has a way of making another person feel special. By smiling, shaking hands, and making eye contact, I showed them my eagerness to speak with them and hear about how they were doing. And by using Hannah's name, I showed that I cared about her enough to remember and use everyone's most favorite word. Dale Carnegie once said that "a person's name is to that person the sweetest and most important sound in any language." If you just try remembering and using people's names, you'll be amazed at the power it has to make them feel special.

Again, I know that these kinds of things don't come easily to everyone. If you're less naturally enthusiastic, then it often helps to imagine yourself in a totally different place. One of the ways I keep my enthusiasm running high is by thinking about Disney World. I think about how I felt the very first time I walked into the Magic Kingdom, and then I try to carry that feeling with me everywhere I go. When this happens, the feeling usually spreads to everyone who crosses paths with me.

If you've never been to the Magic Kingdom, there's this unbelievably positive feeling that happens when you first step through the front gates. You see the castle in the distance, and you feel all the excitement and anticipation of everyone in the crowd. The big clock in the center circle makes you wonder if there's going to be enough time in the day to do everything you're bursting with energy to do. You grin at your favorite Disney characters wandering around and posing for pictures. There's electricity everywhere. You get goose bumps. Your eyes shine.

And that's what being enthusiastic is all about: making someone's eyes shine. It's about doing everything you can to make the other person's moment a positive one—to make them feel like they are the Most Valuable Person.

What does that look like though? How can you do this, especially if you're not the kind of person who is naturally ready to walk up to someone else and speak to them with energy and enthusiasm? It might sound difficult at first, but the more you practice it, the more you'll realize it's the easiest thing in the world: To show (and spread) your enthusiasm, you just need to show the other person that you are genuinely interested in what they have to say.

The more I watched Matthew over the course of his week at camp, the more I realized that this was exactly what made him so magnetic. Yes, he was outgoing and had a great sense of humor, but when he talked to the other kids at camp, he *listened* intently, asked questions, and showed them he heard them and cared about what they had to say.

Think about how difficult this must have been for the new kid in town! He could have looked out at all those kids at camp and recognized that he didn't have any friends, and he could have allowed that to become fear and anxiety. He could have stayed quiet and kept to himself. Instead, he saw a group of unfamiliar faces and said, "You know what? I don't know anyone here, so I might as well be myself." He opened himself up and said, "Hey, this is who I am. This is where I want to be. And this is how I'm going to play."

This level of enthusiasm isn't something that happens overnight. It's a mindset that we all have to grow into. I'm living proof that this growth is possible. Was I the most enthusiastic kid back when I was being picked on every morning on the bus and picked last for everything on the playground? No, I wasn't. Then, I started absorbing the lessons that would lead me to where I am today, and now the enthusiasm flows naturally in everything I do.

A funny thing happens when you do this. You will notice that when you are enthusiastic, the positivity all around you grows. *Enthusiasm is contagious.* The more enthusiasm you give, the more you receive, and the more you receive, the easier it becomes.

3. Choose Courage

I've always wanted to start a story with "Once upon a time," so that's what I'm going to do here. Would that be okay? Okay.

Once upon a time . . . there was a tiger who lived in a jungle. The tiger was dozing in the sun one day when he heard a tiny squeaking sound near his huge front paws. When the tiger opened his eyes, he realized that the sound was coming from the tiniest mouse. Now, it annoyed him to have been woken up from such a nice afternoon nap, and he was also feeling a little snacky, so he picked up one of his huge paws and set it down on the little mouse's tail.

"Please, Mr. Tiger!" the mouse said, quivering with fear. "If you let me go, someday I will return the favor."

The tiger let loose with a roaring laugh. "What could a tiny thing like you ever do for me?"

"I don't know," the mouse admitted. "But one day, you will see."

After thinking about this for a moment, the tiger said, "I could eat you right now if I wanted to, but it's not worth the trouble. You're too small."

With that, he let the mouse go.

Less than a week later, the tiger was out looking for food when something strange and unexpected happened. Suddenly, there was movement under his massive paws, and all at once, he found himself hanging from a tree, swinging upside down inside a trapper's net. He struggled and slashed at the ropes but couldn't free himself. In frustration and fear, he cried out for help.

Somewhere in the distance, the little mouse heard the tiger's cries. He raced toward the sound and discovered the animal who had spared his life. "You see!" the mouse called up to the tiger. "I told you that I would return the favor."

By now, the tiger had started to cry. He didn't believe that there was anything anyone could do to save him. "Go away, little mouse," he said.

But the mouse wasn't having any of that! He climbed up the nearest tree, tiptoed across the rope that was holding the trap, and then began to gnaw away at the net.

At first, the tiger couldn't even bear to open his eyes. But then he felt the bindings begin to loosen. "You're doing it!" he said. "I can't believe it!"

Finally, the mouse had chewed clean through the net, making a hole big enough for the tiger to wriggle through and escape. The tiger plopped to the ground, stretched himself out, and gave a wide smile.

"See?" the mouse said, standing on his hind legs and putting his little paws on his hips. "Even a little mouse can help a tiger."

From that day forward, the tiger and the courageous little mouse were the best of friends.

There are a couple of things I take away from this story. First, courage can come in many forms, and it doesn't matter who you are, what you can do, or how big or small you are; courage is something that you can accept as part of your positive mindset. The other part is that you don't have to be a big, mighty figure to help someone. All you need is the courage to help.

While we're thinking about that part of the moral, let's imagine what it might look like in our everyday lives. Do you know any tigers? I don't mean that literally. I mean it like this: Do you know anyone who is acting out or feeling sad or maybe even being mean to the other kids in school or on the team? Sometimes, when young people are going through tough times (whether it's at home or at school or with their friends), they mask it by being mean. Being mean to other people will make them feel better about themselves, if only for a minute or two.

If we're thinking about these kinds of people as tigers, what can we do to be like the courageous mouse? We can stand up and use empathy! That little mouse had the courage to help a tiger in his time of need. You can help the tigers in your life with some encouragement and support too. Even if the person we're talking about is the best athlete, smartest student, most talented musician—whatever it happens to be—if they're feeling down or acting out, *you* have the power to help them. It takes courage to provide that for someone else, but I know you have it in you!

Okay, but what if this person has been mean to you in the past? As someone with a positive mindset, we also need to have the ability to forgive. Forgiveness is itself an act of courage. If the mouse hadn't forgiven the tiger for laughing at him, he never would have helped him.

It's hard to forgive someone who has been mean to you or you've had an argument or disagreement with. But always remember that the future is more important than what's happened in the past. The future friendship that you could have with this person is far more important. It takes courage to set aside what has happened, look past it, and start or repair the relationship. It takes courage to ask the person, "Is there a reason you're talking to me this way? Is there something I can do to change what's happening here?"

By the way, it works with adults too. If your parents or guardians are having a tough time at home, you can ask them if there's anything you can do to help make their day better. If things aren't going as well for you on the team as you'd like, you could ask for a meeting with your coach and ask if there's anything you could do to get on the field more often. Yes, these things take courage, but again, I know you have it in you!

You know what else is an act of courage? Learning how to laugh at yourself. This doesn't come easily for most people. This is because it's much easier to take yourself too seriously. Even I do it sometimes. When we make a mistake or when someone gives us some constructive criticism, many of us will put up our defenses just like I used to do as a foster kid moving between houses and schools during my childhood. Through all this, if I hadn't been able to develop a sense of humor and laugh at myself once in a while, I'm not sure I would have the coaching career I have today.

Humor is such a powerful and positive tool. It feeds a person's enthusiasm, both for yourself and the people around you. Being able to laugh at yourself will also make other people like you even more. Whenever you can, and whenever it's appropriate, have the courage to be the silly version of yourself.

4. Seek a Mentor

Reshaping your mindset isn't easy. Even with all the lessons and activities in this book, you might find that you need some help from time to time. The best place to find that help is from someone who has been in your shoes, respects what you're trying to do to develop a positive mindset, and cares enough about you to help you get there. This kind of person is someone we call a *mentor*, and believe me, it's never too early in life to find someone who can play that role for you.

For some kids, the mentor is obvious: a parent. But that's not always the case. In my early years, my parents weren't available to be my mentors. My mom led by example, but the way my childhood was, my parents weren't able to be there for me when I needed advice or guidance. I had to seek out mentorship from other adults.

This isn't easy to do, of course. It's hard to ask for help. It takes more of that courage we've been talking about. If we're going to make this change, we first have to accept the idea that it's necessary, even if we think we have all the knowledge we need right now. If you ask someone to be a mentor, you might be surprised by what you have yet to learn! I know it's true for me. I'm an adult, and I still learn so much from the people around me every day.

So, if it isn't a parent (or if you're looking for a mentor *in addition* to a parent), who could you ask? Teachers or coaches can make good mentors, but not all of them are in the best position to serve in this way. The kind of mentor who helps you build a positive mindset is someone who is able to put themselves in your shoes, ask questions and listen, and think beyond the classroom or practice or game. A great mentor helps you learn more about life, about who you are, and helps you become a better person in addition to teaching you math or basketball.

Now I know this one is especially tough. Approaching an adult—especially one who isn't your parent or guardian—to ask for advice or guidance can be a scary idea. But you will be amazed at how positive people can be when you ask them this kind of favor. People *like* to be looked up to, and more than that, they love to help when they are given a chance. Give it a try! Even if the person you approach doesn't have the advice you need, they'll be likely to have some ideas about who else you could ask.

5. Be Ready and Willing to Do More Than Is Asked of You

We've all heard about the importance of hard work, but for me, hard work isn't just about doing everything that's expected of you; it's about doing more.

When I was speaking on this subject in front of a girls' basketball team, I asked one of the players in the front row what this meant to her.

"If your coach tells you that you need to do seven sets of line-touches at the end of practice, what would doing more than is asked of you look like?"

The girl smiled and said, "I'm going to do ten."

Most of us had expected her to say she would do eight, so many of the adults in the room laughed.

"Whoa!" I said. "*Ten sets*? I want you on my team!"

And I wasn't alone in feeling this way! Everyone in the room wanted her on their team. Her willingness to do more than is required not only showed her dedication to her team and teammates, it spread to everyone else too. That level of willingness to do more than is asked of you is such a huge part of developing a positive mindset.

———

I'm going to close on that idea about doing more than is asked of you, because it's another one of those things that we can make a habit by letting it travel the eighteen inches to our hearts. Doing ten sets of line-touches once is great, but this kind of thing doesn't become a part of your mindset until you find yourself looking for opportunities to do more in *everything* that's required of you. When you're not even thinking about how you're doing a few extra minutes of studying every night, staying after practice to work on some things, cleaning your room without being asked, getting up a little earlier so you can work on the plays in this book—*that's* when you'll know that you have made this positive mindset a part of who you are.

Just like with anything in life, the process starts by taking that first step. Write down those positive qualities. Look for opportunities to show and spread your enthusiasm. Show your courage every day. Find a mentor. And always, always be ready and willing to do more than is asked of you. That may sound like a lot, but I know you have it in you!

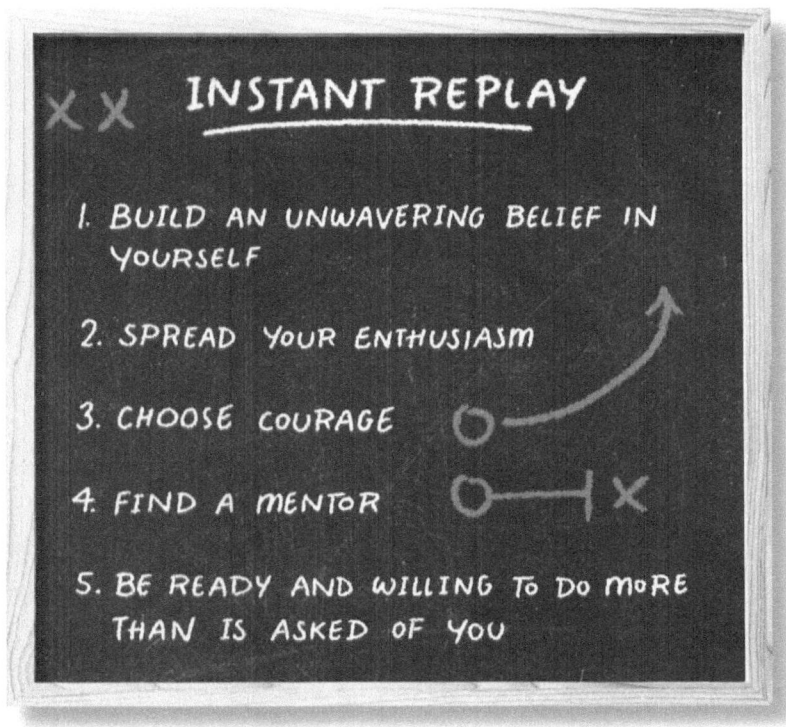

CHALK TALK #5

Five Plays for Dealing with Adversity

---

*Obstacles don't have to stop you. If you run into a wall,
don't turn around and give up. Figure out how to climb it,
go through it, or work around it.*

—Michael Jordan

It's easy enough to be positive with yourself and everyone around you when life is going great. But life can sometimes be challenging. We all face some setbacks every once in a while. It's not a question of *if* it will happen; it's a question of how you deal with it when it does.

In my life, the kinds of challenging situations we're talking about here have come in many different forms. I grew up without my parents and spent some years in foster care. My teen years were full of bad decisions that put me on the wrong path. I've met some doubters and some struggles in building my business. But when I think back on my tough times, there is one period that stands out above all the others.

There was a time when my coaching business was doing really well—so well that some major partners approached me with an offer to grow the business into something bigger and better. As a first step, the business moved into a brand-new facility. It felt good to be able to say, "Hey, this is my building." And because I wanted it to be a top-notch place for kids to come learn and play, I spent everything I had in my savings account to make sure that we had the best turf and equipment available at the time.

A few days after I'd spent my last dime on that athletic training center, a close family member was diagnosed with cancer. I was devastated. And I shifted my focus to helping take care of them. Battling cancer was an incredibly emotional challenge for them, for our families, and for me. In our situation, the medical bills came at the exact wrong time too. My lowest point was a time when I went to the grocery store just to buy milk, and my debit card was declined because I didn't have the three dollars it cost to buy a gallon. Soon after, I received a call that my car—a new car that I had been so proud to be able to afford for the first time in my life—was going to be repossessed.

There I was, feeling like I'd gone from the top of the world in my business to the absolute lowest point. I could have folded up shop right then. Could have given up on my business, given up on trying to make ends meet, and just felt hopeless about what my family member was going through. For a while, it was tempting to give up. But then I remembered the plays I'm going to share with you in this Chalk Talk, and everything changed.

The first thing I did was to take a side job to help keep the lights on at home and in my business. That job was as a courier. I was delivering packages to businesses in downtown Pittsburgh. One day, I delivered a package to someone who knew me from my sports programs. I had coached one of his kids in a flag football league.

"Coach Dave?" he said, surprised to see me in a courier's uniform. "What are you doing here?"

I didn't know how to answer. I was flustered and embarrassed about someone I knew learning that I'd had to take a side job just to make ends meet. But you know what? That embarrassment came from a sense of selfishness. It meant I was only thinking about me—how I would look or how people would think of me—and had lost sight of *why* I was doing this second job.

After work that night, I went back home and told myself that I had to swallow my pride and do whatever it takes to make sure we had the money to pay for my family member's treatment. I reorganized my priorities and my focus on what it was that really mattered in life. At my lowest moment, I learned that there are more important things than pride to fight for.

Once I had my mindset right again, I knew I had to take action to fix how things were going and help the family get through the obstacles we were facing. It was a long and difficult road back to where I am today, but I'm living proof (and I'm happy to say that my family member is also living proof) that with a positive mindset, there's no challenge so big that you can't overcome.

So, how can you deal with adversity, just like I did? Here's the playbook:

1. Look for the Light

People often ask me how I always stay so positive. It's hard for some people to imagine how a person can be so upbeat even during the most challenging times. The first thing I do is remind myself that there is always light at the end of the tunnel. For me, whenever I'm dealing with adversity or feeling down, I tell myself that it's only temporary. It's that old saying, "This too shall pass."

When my family member was dealing with their most difficult point during their battle with cancer, I said, "This too shall pass, and you're going to come out at the end of it as a different, better person." We each accepted this as reality, and when we did this, it became a part of our positive mindset. That positivity carried us through every day, and ultimately, it helped guide us to that light at the end of the tunnel.

The power of looking for the light, and of "This too shall pass" is that it helps you stay more focused on the positives rather than getting wrapped up in the negatives that are happening at the moment. Even in our lowest moments, we can take comfort that they won't last forever—not if we don't let them.

Whatever you're experiencing right now, it's only temporary. It will pass. And there will be better days ahead.

2. Answer the Call

An important piece to remember about the wisdom that "This too shall pass" is that the better days will come sooner if you take action. The work you will need to put in might be tough, but sometimes we have to do things we don't want to do just to get through it. When you're feeling down—maybe you're having difficulty in school or you had a bad day at practice or you had an argument with a friend—it's so easy to just sit in your room and feel sorry for yourself. It can be a good thing to be alone and think your way through things for a little while. But eventually, it's time to get out there and take action. If you want to get yourself back on a positive track, then it's up to you to answer the call.

ACTION PLAN: Answering the Call

Take a few minutes to think about a challenge you're facing right now. It could be something at school, in sports, with friends, or at home. Now, let's create your personal action plan to help you move toward that light at the end of the tunnel.

Today: Write down three specific actions you can take TODAY to start addressing your challenge. These should be small, doable steps that you can accomplish in the next twenty-four hours.

1. _____
2. _____
3. _____

This Week: Now, think about what you can do THIS WEEK to keep your momentum going. What are four actions that might take a little more time or preparation but that you can complete in the next seven days?

1. _____
2. _____
3. _____
4. _____

Until You Reach the Light: Finally, write down three bigger actions that might take more time but will help you reach that light at the end of the tunnel. These are your longer-term goals that will help you overcome this challenge completely.

1. _____
2. _____
3. _____

Remember: Just writing down these actions isn't enough—you need to commit to DOING them. Put this list somewhere you'll see it every day, like taped to your bathroom mirror or inside your school notebook. Each time you complete an action, check it off and celebrate that small victory. You're answering the call, one step at a time!

3. Don't Let the Doubters Bring You Down

Adversity isn't always about an event in your life, but about people telling you that you aren't good enough or that you won't succeed.

Around the time I first started my business with my best friend, Chris, my loudest doubter sent me an email to try to discourage me from what I was doing. In the email, he basically said that I wouldn't succeed because I was lazy and didn't have the knowledge or work ethic needed to start a business. It was the most discouraging thing I have ever read. And it really got to me for a while. It made me question my decision to start a business. Made me question my identity. Made me think, "You know what? He's probably right." I had never coached before. What did I know about coaching kids?

First, I was hurt. And then, I became filled with anger. When you're dealing with doubters or naysayers, it's so easy to get trapped by anger because it helps you feel better about what's happening in your life or about what that other person said. But anger is just as destructive as doubt. How did I get past the anger? I used it to fuel my motivation to succeed.

If you're feeling doubtful or angry, it's going to be much more difficult to ignore your doubters. When that happens, the easy way out is to stop caring. If we lose sight of the light and the sense that this too shall pass, we start saying and thinking, "I don't care" about everything. That can lead to a lot of negativity. Our schoolwork suffers. We might start being mean to the people at home or the other kids at school. We might quit on our teams or clubs. Because if we don't care, why would anyone else care, right?

If you find yourself thinking like this, then you know for sure that you're dealing with doubt. You can allow that doubt to dig you further into the hole of adversity, or you can turn it around and use it as motivation to dig your way out. Ultimately, the choice is yours.

When I finally put that email behind me, I thought about how there were other people around me—Chris especially—who were supportive and positive and knew I could succeed. In your own life, I bet you have a few of those people too. During the challenging times, it's always a good idea to lean on those people.

4. Be True to Yourself

Back when I was in sixth grade, the kids on the bus were not kind to me. Some of the older kids were so mean to me that, even when there were open seats on the school bus, they would make me sit in the middle aisle between the seats. In fact, I had to use my saxophone case as a seat.

Every day for what felt like months, I faced the same thing. It got to the point where I wanted to be anyone else but me. I thought, "Why me? Why are these kids singling me out like this? What's wrong with me?"

Even as a sixth grader, I kind of knew the answer. I was new at the school. I was a foster kid. I was lonely and didn't have many friends. The fact that I felt ashamed of these things made me an easy target. I know there are a lot of kids out there today who are asking themselves that same question: "Why me?"

When we start asking this question of ourselves, the easy response is to just ignore everything and give up. We might even start pretending to be someone we aren't. In either case, the pain causes us to not be true to ourselves.

The path out of this isn't an easy one. Remember all those positive things we wrote down about ourselves in the last Chalk Talk? Whenever we start feeling that self-doubt and feeling sorry for ourselves, it's usually a great idea to get out that list and read it over—not just once, not just twice, but every day! It can happen in the morning after we wake up, just before bed each night, or whenever we're feeling especially down. The more time we spend on thinking about those positive qualities, the easier it is to stay positive in the face of adversity.

Those tough times are also a great opportunity to lean on our chosen mentor. Just like everyone else in the world, your mentor has faced challenges—maybe his/hers are similar to the ones you're going through right now! This person is going to be in a great position to give you the kind of advice and help you need to take that next step on your journey toward the light at the end of the tunnel. Along the way, if we believe in ourselves, and if we lean on the support of the people who love and value us, even this too shall pass.

In my situation on the bus as a sixth grader, I had just fallen into the trap of pretending to be someone I wasn't when, one day, an eighth grader stood up and spoke up for me. "Hey, Dave," he said. "You can sit here by me."

Now this was a big deal for more than one reason. Not only

did it prevent me from having to deal with being picked on that day; the other kids on the bus really looked up to that eighth grader. When he stood up for me, it changed everything about how the other kids treated me.

I'm not sure why that eighth grader did what he did, but that one brief, seemingly minor step he took to show everyone on the bus that I deserved kindness just like everyone else changed how every ride on the bus went after that. It changed how I looked at going to school. And most importantly, it made me realize that I was someone of value. It helped me take that first giant step toward being true to myself, and when I started doing that, the light at the end of the tunnel just kept getting bigger and bigger.

There's another part of this play that you might have noticed in that story. Sometimes, when you see someone else who's dealing with adversity, you can help in bigger ways than you realize. You don't even have to do that much . . . Just speak up.

5. Find Your Fans

When you're facing challenges, or when the doubters are getting you down, that's when it's most important to turn to the people in your life who are positive, who love you, and who want to support you. For many young people, it's about turning to friends and family. For others, the support system might come from places you least expect.

Back in second grade, I had just come out of the foster care system, and my aunt and uncle had become my legal guardians. They enrolled me into a new elementary school. I was so scared about going to this school because I didn't know anyone—not any of the teachers or the students. In those first few days at school, I did what a lot of kids do when they're feeling this kind of fear: I didn't talk much. In fact, I didn't talk at all. Can you imagine that? Me, Coach Dave, *not talking*? It seems crazy to think about. But it's true. I talked so little that the teachers started to think I had a learning disability.

You know who recognized that I was just scared and unsure of myself? You know who became one of the most impactful and influential people in my life? It wasn't a teacher. It wasn't a coach. It wasn't a sports figure. It was my elementary school custodian.

Mr. Swan was in his late fifties or early sixties. He was the coolest person I had ever met in my young life. All of the kids, when they saw Mr. Swan, would go running to him and give him a hug. He would smile and ask them how they were doing and have conversations with them. As the kid who was scared to talk to anyone, I would mostly just see this from afar. Truthfully, it made me a little bit upset at first, because I wanted to be one of those kids. I wanted to feel that attention and appreciation from Mr. Swan.

Well, one day, while I was walking back to my home room from gym class, I heard a voice. "Hey, David! How are you today?"

I looked over and couldn't believe that it was Mr. Swan. How did he know my name? I had never talked to him before. But you know what happened? I ran over to Mr. Swan, and I didn't even think twice about it. All it took was for him to acknowledge me, to use my name, and to smile. Just like all those other kids, I ran up and gave him a hug.

Mr. Swan simply asked me how I liked the school so far. I heard myself talking to him more openly than I had with anyone since I first moved in with my aunt and uncle. It didn't make me start talking to anyone and everyone in school, but it did make me feel like I had a sense of belonging, that someone appreciated me, that someone *saw* me.

That simple act of kindness made everything about that year better for me. It speaks so much to the power of so many of the things we've been discussing so far in this book: what you can achieve with simple kindnesses; what happens when you use someone's name; how important it is to smile and be positive, to ask questions, and to genuinely listen.

Mr. Swan became an unexpected fan of mine, and I was a fan of his. Over the years, as I grew and changed and faced new challenges, I would find other fans. Mrs. Peel asking me if I would have breakfast with her before school one day. My best friend and first business partner, Chris, who saw through all the struggles I was having and recognized me for the person I was and the person I was capable of becoming. The example set by Roberto Clemente, who has always been a role model, that hero whose good deeds have inspired me to be who I am as a coach and a person. The group of three friends from my neighborhood as a kid, who, no matter what was happening, were always up for a game of Wiffle Ball or tackle football in their yard, sleepovers on weekends, or BMX rides as far as we could peddle.

There's an old saying that if you want to fly with the eagles, you have to stop swimming with the ducks. Think of the ducks as the people who are always quacking and complaining and being negative. Your support system is that group of eagles who help you fly. Surround yourself with positive people who share your passions, who believe in you, and who see you for who you are, and there will never be a tough time that you can't overcome.

You Will Get Through It

When we face challenging times, there is no easy solution. The five plays that make up this Chalk Talk take hard work, consistency, and determination. When the times are tough, it's just so much easier to get bogged down by negative thinking than it is to surround yourself with positive thoughts, actions, and people.

There was a time after high school when I was unemployed, failing college, staying up late every night searching for answers, ordering any get-rich-quick system I could afford to buy. And every time I tried one of those easy ways out, it failed. This was a huge part of why my biggest doubter's email had such an impact on me: He was partly right! I had failed at many things, and I hadn't given the people in my life much reason to believe that my new business as a youth coach would be any different.

But then, thanks to Chris's words of encouragement, thanks to the guidance from the fans I found in my own life, and thanks to a positive attitude, a determination to remain true to myself, and to my work ethic, I found the happiness and fulfillment that had been missing from my life. I am living proof that no matter what you're going through, if you take action on these five plays, and you're determined to get through it, you will get through it.

INSTANT REPLAY

1. LOOK FOR THE LIGHT

2. ANSWER THE CALL

3. DON'T LET THE DOUBTERS BRING YOU DOWN

4. BE TRUE TO YOURSELF

5. FIND YOUR FANS

CHALK TALK #6

Five Plays to Make the Most of Your Day

---

*The difference between ordinary and extraordinary
is that little extra.*

–Jimmy Johnson

"A new day, a new opportunity." This is how I think about each day when I first wake up in the morning. To me, this is one of the most powerful things I do every day. It puts me into a positive mindset right away, but it also helps me remember that I might make mistakes today—actually, just like anyone, I make mistakes pretty much every day—but if I recognize and learn from them, then it creates a new opportunity to get just a little bit better as a person.

This is what's so great about every new day. No matter what happens, progress or setbacks, it's always a new opportunity to learn and grow.

I've been running youth sports camps for over twenty years now, and one thing I've noticed is that the kids who get the most out of each day are the ones who have established positive daily routines. These routines help them show up ready to learn, play, and grow—both as athletes and as people.

Let me tell you about a camper named Jason who attended one of my summer programs a few years ago. On the first day, Jason arrived late, without breakfast, looking tired and unprepared. He struggled to keep up with the activities and seemed frustrated all day. After camp, I pulled him aside for a quick chat about how a few small changes to his morning routine might help him enjoy camp more.

The next morning, Jason arrived fifteen minutes early, had eaten breakfast, and brought a water bottle. The difference was incredible! He participated enthusiastically in every activity, encouraged his teammates, and wore a smile all day. When I asked what changed, he said, "I just did what you suggested, Coach Dave. I got up earlier, ate breakfast, and made sure I was ready before I left the house. It wasn't even that hard!"

That's the power of small daily habits. They might seem insignificant on their own, but together, they can transform your entire day—and eventually, your life.

So far, most of the plays we've discussed have been about your character or your mindset. But these plays are a little different. These plays are all about the actions you can take to make every day more positive and productive. To the adults reading this, you can do these things too! In fact, these five plays are a great opportunity for you to lead by example. You might just find that they make as much of a difference in your day as they do for the young person you're supporting.

So, how can we start each day in a way that will ensure we're making the most of it? Here's the playbook:

1. Find Reward in an Early Rise

You know that old saying about how the early bird gets the worm? Who wants worms anyway? Fortunately, if you're not a bird, there are much better rewards for getting up early.

I know, I know. This is a tough one for some people. And you know how I know? Because it's a tough one for me! These days, I wake up at 6:30 every morning. For some of you who have to get up to catch the bus to school, that might actually sound kind of late, but believe me, it's plenty early for me. The point here isn't about the exact time when you wake up each morning; it's about being consistent with the time you wake up, and also to set that wakeup time to be early enough so you can be fully awake, fully alert, and ready to have a positive start to your day by the time the morning bell rings at school (or on weekends, by the time your first activity starts).

It took practice for me to be able to do this every day, because waking up early is not something that I'm naturally built to do. I always wake up so groggy that getting out of bed is almost painful. It wasn't easy at first; but it takes a while to develop a new habit. Each day that I kept to the routine, it became a little easier.

Let me share a trick that helped me become an early riser. When I was first trying to establish this habit, I would set two alarms—one that would give me just enough time to get ready if I got up immediately, and another thirty minutes earlier. I placed the earlier alarm across the room so I had to physically get out of bed to turn it off. Even if I crawled back into bed after turning it off (which I sometimes did!), I had already broken the seal of sleep. It became much easier to actually get up when the second alarm went off.

If you think of every day as a new opportunity, then even the days when you have nothing on the schedule, you can accomplish some important things. Now that I start every day at 6:30, I get so much more done—not just in the morning, but throughout the day. Because I get so much more done, I feel good about myself and what I've accomplished each day.

I'm going to ask you another thing that might be challenging. I know it was difficult for me for a while. I'm going to ask you to take responsibility for waking yourself up in the morning. If you can set an alarm and get yourself up instead of relying on a parent or guardian or sibling to wake you, then you will be starting each day by being accountable for yourself. Why is this important? Because it helps you be accountable for completing the other Four Plays to Make the Most of Your Day!

2. Hydration + Nutrition = Rejuvenation

Whenever I share this second play with people, they look at me like, "Coach Dave, what are you talking about?" But if you can visualize this equation each morning, and you make it a part of your daily routine, you won't believe how much better you'll feel.

Let's start with hydration. Water has so many benefits, and most of us don't drink nearly enough of it. You know how I make sure to get enough water each day? By getting ahead of the game first thing in the morning.

Right after I wake up, I drink sixteen ounces of water. Just to make sure I don't forget, it's the very first thing I do once I get myself out of bed. Not only does this set me up to meet the daily recommendation of sixty-four ounces per day, it also helps me wake up. When you sleep, you lose hydration. When you wake up, you're going to feel a little run-down. Believe it or not, this is a big part of why you're sometimes so groggy in the morning. If you take care of that dehydration right away, you'll be awake and alert that much quicker.

Did you know that your brain is about 75 percent water? When you're dehydrated, your brain actually functions differently. Studies have shown that even mild dehydration can impact your mood, energy level, and ability to think clearly. This is especially important for students who need to concentrate in class all day.

Then, over the course of the day, if you remember to keep drinking water, you'll feel healthier and more energetic than ever.

Now let's talk about nutrition. This is something I've had on my mind for a long time, partly because my family has a history of high blood pressure. The first time I had a high blood pressure reading while visiting the doctor, I decided that I had to start paying closer attention to what I was eating. Since then, I've been eating oatmeal with flax seeds every morning, and you know what? My blood pressure went down to normal in just two weeks.

Now, I know you're a little young to be thinking about blood pressure, so that's not what I'm asking you to do. What I'm asking you to do is much simpler: Don't skip meals! While you're growing and developing as a person, every meal is incredibly important. And that includes breakfast!

Your brain needs fuel just like your body does. When you skip breakfast, you're asking your brain to work without giving it the energy it needs. It's like trying to drive a car with an empty gas tank—you might move a little bit, but you won't get very far!

We've all heard it time and time again: Breakfast is the most important meal of the day. It's what helps us recover when we wake up, what gets our minds going, what fuels us through the morning. If all that's true, then why is it so easy to skip breakfast? Even I sometimes have to force myself to eat breakfast. With my schedule, especially in the summer when I'm getting up at dawn to set up my camps, it's so easy to want to just skip the nutrition and head out the door with a coffee. I've had to adapt to this routine over the years. Now if I absolutely can't have my oatmeal with flax, I'm making sure to take some fruit with me or make a smoothie that I can drink in the car on the way to camp. All those nutrients get me to lunch, when I have a little more time to refuel.

Your schedule during the school year might look pretty rushed in the morning too. But the message is the same—and it's especially important for young people who are still growing and learning so many new things every day. Even if you're running late, you can grab a banana and a protein bar. It sounds so simple and so obvious, and yet too many people look past this play. If you make sure to drink water and eat breakfast every morning, you'll feel so much better every day.

3. Put Down the Screen, Pick Up Your Feet

For a long time, the first thing I did every morning—before I even got out of bed—was to pick up my phone and start scrolling. First thing, I would check my text messages, emails, and Facebook timeline. I know there are younger people than me who make a habit of checking Instagram and TikTok and a bunch of other social media networks I'm not as familiar with.

At some point, you know what I discovered? I figured out that starting my day by burying myself in what was happening on my phone screen made me less ready to approach my day in the real world. Keeping up with all that messaging—especially on social media—can be stressful and emotionally draining. That's no way to treat yourself before you even get out of bed!

There's some fascinating science behind why starting your day with screen time can be problematic. The blue light emitted by phones and tablets actually suppresses melatonin, a hormone that helps regulate your sleep-wake cycle. So when you look at your screen first thing in the morning, you're confusing your body's natural rhythms.

These days, when I get up and start my daily routine, my phone stays right where I left it overnight: charging on the nightstand. I make a point not to look at it until I'm ready to go into my office and officially start my workday. Whenever you decide to allow yourself to look at your screen for the first time, it's usually best to at least wait until after you've had breakfast.

By the way, this play is great for kids and adults alike. Whoever you are or whatever you do with your days, you don't need to look at your phone first thing in the morning. Whatever is waiting for you on that screen can wait until you've had a chance to wake up, organize your mind, and prepare yourself for the great day ahead.

Okay, so we've put our screens down, now let's think about every chance we can get to pick up our feet! When you're a young person in school, it's important to take advantage of every opportunity for physical activity. If you focus on looking for chances to be active, it will become a part of who you are and help you grow into a happier and healthier adult. Whether you're at recess, in gym class, an after-school sport, or you just need to make time to move your body on your own after school, never miss an opportunity to get your heart pumping.

Did you know that just twenty minutes of physical activity can boost your brain power for up to two hours afterward? That's right—exercise doesn't just make your body stronger; it actually helps your brain function better too! When you exercise, your body increases blood flow to the brain and releases chemicals that enhance memory, focus, and problem-solving abilities.

Every day, I drive to North Park (which is a popular recreation area with a lake near my house), put my headphones on, and listen to my favorite playlist while I walk. Some days, I have time to walk all the way around the lake. Other days, maybe it's just a mile or two. Sometimes, it's so cold that I can only handle being out there for a few minutes. The distance and time don't matter as much as the routine.

The kind of physical activity you choose to do doesn't matter either. Maybe you get today's exercise by playing with your dog in the yard. Maybe you can walk down the street to a friend's house to shoot baskets, jump on a trampoline, or throw the football around. Having a routine doesn't necessarily mean doing the same thing every day; it can mean making sure you get the same benefits every day—and all physical activity has benefits.

So with this play, let's learn to take a break from the screens and make movement and exercise a priority. Then the screen time can be the reward. The more you move, the more your brain starts functioning in a powerful, motivating way. It's healthy for your mind as much as your body. If you find the time to move (and to play!), then you will feel happier and more fulfilled throughout the day.

4. Have Fun with It!

Every morning, I get the water running in the shower, then I turn on a Bluetooth speaker and start blaring my salsa and reggaeton music. I have an app that pipes in a radio station based in Puerto Rico, so I'm listening to the same songs I would be if I was on vacation. For you, the music might be different. It doesn't matter what you listen to—music, the news, podcasts. What matters is that it needs to be something that energizes you.

Music has an incredible power to affect our mood and energy level. Scientists have found that upbeat music can increase your heart rate, release endorphins (those feel-good chemicals in your brain), and even synchronize your body's rhythms to the beat. In other words, the right music can literally get your body and mind moving in the right direction!

I keep my dance music going while I floss and brush my teeth, and even keep it cranked up while I'm getting dressed.

Speaking of getting dressed, here's something you might think about doing: Whenever I have a program scheduled for that day, I make sure to dress the part. For me, that means making sure that everything I'm wearing is clean, goes well together, and looks presentable. Whenever I go into a school, I'm wearing a collared shirt that's well pressed, my warmups are clean, my shoes are neat and perfectly tied, and so on.

There's an important message here, one that sticks with me in particular because I wasn't always able to afford the nicest clothes: It doesn't matter the brand of your clothes or how much they cost; what matters is that they are clean, presentable, and you show that you care about your choices.

Like it or not, we're all judged on how we appear. Be your creative self and wear what you want to wear, but make sure it fits, it isn't wrinkled, and it's clean. Think about your shoes too. Are they clean? Are the laces tied neatly? Do they (and your clothes, and you) smell good?

The other side to this lesson is that when you look good, you feel good. This might seem like a small piece of the puzzle, but believe me, it goes a long way toward the attitude you will carry throughout the day.

5. Recite Your Positive Affirmations

You remember the first play from Chalk Talk #4: Five Plays for a Positive Mindset? Here's a reminder: It was about building an unwavering belief in yourself. You remember how we took the time to write down all those positive things about yourself. We called those "positive affirmations." Yes, we wrote them down the first time because they're useful when you're thinking about how to build that positive mindset, and they're especially useful whenever you're going through a difficult time. But there's no reason that those positive affirmations can't be a part of our daily routine. In fact, so far, we've been talking mostly about our physical health, but this last play is important for another big part of who we are: our mental health.

The science behind positive affirmations is fascinating. When you repeat positive statements about yourself, you're actually creating new neural pathways in your brain. These pathways make it easier for your brain to think positively in the future. It's like creating a shortcut for positive thoughts!

Just like you, I have taken the time to write down my positive affirmations. And I have found that, whether I do this as part of my morning routine, right before bed at night, or both, when I take the time to read through and remind myself about those positive affirmations, I feel better about myself, about my day, and about anything and everything going on in my life.

Here's what my daily affirmations look like:

- "I'm Coach Dave Gray, and I choose to be positive. Every day, I will make a difference in the lives of those around me."
- "I believe in myself and believe that I can do whatever I set my mind to, as long as I put in the hard work and give 100 percent of my effort."
- "Even when I am going through something negative or have had a challenging experience, I choose to be a positive person."
- "I recognize that I have shortcomings, but they are a part of who I am, and that authentic version of who I am is worth celebrating. Along with my shortcomings, I have many important skills that I can and do use to improve my life and the lives of the people around me."
- "Tomorrow, like today, I will use all of these qualities and skills to shine my light on others, to make them see their worth and feel good about themselves."

You and I are different people, so your affirmations might look a little different from mine. What matters most is that the message should always be positive. While I recite mine at the beginning and end of each day, you can recite yours at any time that works best for you. Some people I know like to do theirs right before bed. Others will think about it silently whenever they have a free moment during the day. Sometimes, it's really useful to return to it whenever you're experiencing self-doubt.

There is great power to writing these affirmations and repeating them regularly. The more you return to them, the more you develop that positive mindset, and the more positive your thinking becomes. Just like consistent sleep, hydration and nutrition, physical activity, and having fun and looking good can help your physical health, spending time on your affirmations can do wonders for your mental health.

Making These Plays a Part of Your Life

I'll finish by coming back to where we started: I know that some of these plays are going to be difficult. Not everyone takes to them naturally. But just like any of the other plays in this book, if you dedicate yourself to them, they will eventually become a routine, and when they become a routine, they eventually become a part of who you are. I used to have to remind myself to follow them, but now, I do them without even having to think about it. And the same can be true for you, as long as you stick to it.

Remember Jason from the beginning of this Chalk Talk? By the end of the two-week camp, he had completely transformed his daily routine. His parents told me they couldn't believe the change in him—not just at camp, but at home too. He was more energetic, more positive, and more helpful around the house. All from implementing these simple plays to make the most of his day.

There will be days when you miss some plays or have some setbacks. Don't let that discourage you! Like anything in life, this is a process. Keep focused on the process and eventually these plays will be as natural to you as they have become for me. You will think more positively, be happier and healthier, and your energy will spread to the people around you.

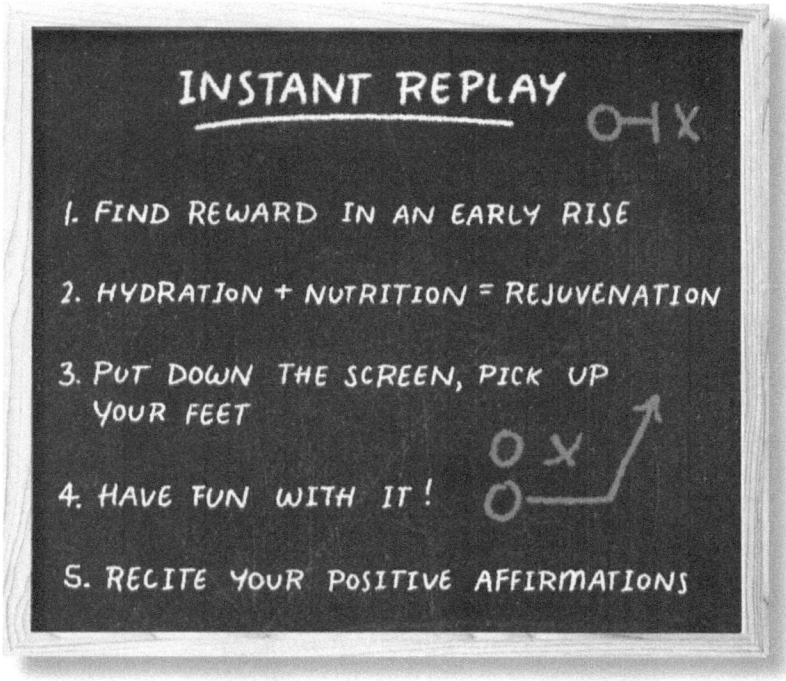

CHALK TALK #7

Five Plays to Make a Positive Impression on Your Coaches and Teachers

---

Your talent determines what you can do. Your motivation determines how much you're willing to do. Your attitude determines how well you do it.

–Lou Holtz

B ack in high school, one of the things I was proudest of was being on the football team. Every summer, our coach would hold voluntary workouts, which meant that even though you didn't have to go to them, it would be better if you did. The summer between my junior and senior year, I chose not to go to them. I guess you could say I hadn't yet learned all of the lessons that make me the person I am today...

Back then, I made the mistake of thinking that my past performance on the field meant that I would definitely be a starter. I was an incoming senior, after all, and there was just no question my coach would give me that honor. So instead of going to voluntary workouts, I spent that summer relaxing with friends.

You can probably see where this is going...

While I was hanging out with friends, other players were taking their responsibility to the team seriously. They went to every open gym. They lifted weights and worked on their speed and endurance every day. They ate the right things, got to bed early, woke up early, and reflected on all those positive daily habits that can lead to improvement as a player and a person. To do all this, they had to sacrifice some of the fun things that I was experiencing that summer. But to them, staying focused on football and their commitment to the team was more important.

Can you guess whether I was named a starter as a senior?

When the first game of the season arrived, I was shocked to find my name on the second string. I approached my coach after practice, certain there must have been some mistake. "Coach," I said, "I was a starter last year. I know this position better than anyone else on the team."

My coach looked at me with disappointment. "Dave," he said, "while you were enjoying your summer, Gabriel was here every day working to get better. He outperformed you in practice, showed more commitment to the team, and earned that starting position. The question isn't why he's starting—it's why you thought you deserved to start without putting in the work."

That moment was a wake-up call I've never forgotten. I learned that past performance doesn't guarantee future success, that positions are earned through consistent effort, and that the impression you make on coaches through your actions speaks louder than any words or past achievements.

This brings us to my first lesson to you before we jump into our five plays: If you want to be the kind of person who makes a great impression on their coaches and teachers, then first you need to take care of today. Today, you need to do all the things necessary to improve yourself as a player, student, and person, so that tomorrow, you can wake up and do it all again.

That's the thing about sports (and life!): There is no such thing as a finished product. If you're always taking care of today, then you know that you have spent your time becoming a better version of yourself. If you're preparing for tryouts, then the mindset has to be to keep working to improve, keep trying to become a better version of the player who is competing for that position. If you're looking to become a better student, then spend each day putting in the work your teachers expect of you, learn all that you can, and then take the next steps to learn even more.

I've spent more than two decades coaching young athletes, and I've noticed something consistent across all sports and age groups: The players who make the best impression aren't always the most naturally talented. They're the ones who consistently demonstrate certain qualities that make coaches and teachers want to invest time and energy in them.

Think about it from a coach's perspective. When you're responsible for a team of fifteen to twenty young athletes, who are you going to spend the most time helping? The player with natural talent who shows up late and unprepared, or the player who might not be as naturally gifted but consistently demonstrates dedication, enthusiasm, and a willingness to learn? The answer is obvious—coaches invest in players who show they're willing to invest in themselves.

Before we jump into the plays, I have a few questions for you to think about:

- Are you taking care of every day?
- Are you preparing for tomorrow?

- Are you demonstrating that you are willing to go the extra mile?
- Are you willing to put in the hard work even when no one's watching?

I hope that your answer to all of those questions is "yes," because to be successful, you have to make a commitment to practice hard, and then make that commitment into a habit. Once you reach that point where hard work and commitment become habits, you will begin to show your best potential on and off the field.

How do we turn that potential into a great impression on your coaches and teachers? Here's the playbook:

1. Be on Time and Be Prepared

One thing you'll notice about the plays in this Chalk Talk is that they're all about the things we can control. What do I mean by that? What I mean is that we can't control the decisions the coach is going to make about who they will choose to play a role on their team. But what we can control is our own actions, and what that coach will see when they watch us perform.

Let me give you a coach's perspective. If I'm picking a team, yes, I want good athletes, but more than that, I want the kids who are willing to put in the work to get better and to contribute to the team. After more than twenty-five years of coaching, I've noticed something: The players who are willing to work hard and do whatever it takes to contribute to the team are easy to spot.

I can usually tell which players are truly committed within the first five minutes of practice. How? By looking at who arrived early, who has all their equipment ready, whose attention is focused on instructions, and who responds first when I ask for volunteers. These aren't just minor details—they're indicators of a player's approach to everything they do.

If we're thinking about controlling only the things we can control, what's the first thing that comes to mind? For me, it's getting there on time. Remember, your coach's or teacher's impression begins when practice or class starts. If you can show up early—and maybe even be the first person on the field or in the gym or through the door—then this tells your coach or teacher that you are someone who cares about this team or class. Better yet, if you're always on time—and whenever possible, even early—then it shows your coach or teacher that you are willing and able to be a leader.

I remember coaching a basketball team where one player, Diego, consistently arrived twenty minutes early to every practice. He didn't make a show of it or expect special recognition—he simply used that time to work on his shooting or ball-handling skills. About halfway through the season, I noticed something interesting: Other players started showing up early too. Without saying a word, Diego had established a new standard for the team through his actions alone.

That's just the external benefit to always being on time; there's an internal benefit too. Have you ever been late to a tryout or a practice or class? How do you feel when that happens? You're scrambling around, probably a little embarrassed because everyone else has already started and you don't even know where you're supposed to be. That embarrassment probably causes you to lose focus, make mistakes, and miss out on truly learning what you need to know in order to succeed. Being late negatively affects everything.

Have you ever heard that old saying that "being early is on time, being on time is late, and being late is unacceptable"? No matter what your goals are, and no matter what success looks like to you, first, just make sure to be on time.

You might have noticed that there's a second part to this play: Be prepared. What do I mean by "be prepared?" I'm not talking about coming into the tryout with notes and a checklist. I'm talking about making sure you have all of your equipment, that your shoes are laced up tight, and that your uniform or practice attire is clean and ready. In a classroom setting, I'm talking about showing up with your books, writing utensils, computer/tablet, or any other materials you may need, and having your homework ready to hand in. Be ready to show your teacher that you have done the reading and are ready to learn more.

Whether you have to pause the practice to tie your shoe or adjust your equipment—or you have to interrupt class while you search for something you were supposed to bring—not being ready shows that you haven't taken the time and energy to be prepared for that practice, game, or class. Coaches and teachers remember that kind of thing. Those are the little points that add up and can make all the difference in the impression you're leaving. Out of all the plays in this Chalk Talk, these little points are also the easiest to control. Always be on time, and always be prepared.

2. Greet Your Coaches and Teammates

Remember Play #2 from Chalk Talk #4? I hope so, but just in case, I'll save you from having to flip back a few pages. That play was called "Spread Your Enthusiasm," and one of the biggest takeaway messages is that people really appreciate it when you greet them, and they especially like it when you use their name. It's like Dale Carnegie said, a person's name is to them "the sweetest and most important sound in any language."

This principle applies powerfully in sports and educational settings. Think about your coach's or teacher's perspective—they might interact with dozens or even hundreds of students or athletes each day. When you take the initiative to greet them personally, you immediately stand out from the crowd.

I remember coaching at a large soccer camp where we had over two hundred kids. On the second day, a twelve-year-old named Tyler approached me at the beginning of the session, looked me in the eye, shook my hand, and said, "Good morning, Coach Dave! I'm excited for today's drills." That simple, ten-second interaction made such an impression that I still remember it years later. Throughout the camp, I found myself paying extra attention to Tyler's progress and offering him additional coaching.

At every practice or game, if you always greet your coaches and teammates, and you use their names when you do, then you will immediately make an impression. If you also show your enthusiasm in the greeting, then the impression only grows.

As a coach, I make a point to greet every single person in my program, whether it's the participants or their parents or guardians or little sister or grandma or grandpa. I'll say something like, "Hi (and then I use their name), welcome to practice!" It sounds like such a small thing, but you won't believe what a difference it makes to greet someone with enthusiasm while also showing them that you care enough about them to remember and use their name.

At your next practice, I want you to do the same thing. Just greeting the people at practice (and in school, and everywhere you go) is going to open doors of opportunity for you that you never thought possible. This kind of thing speaks volumes about your character, which is something your coaches will immediately notice, and your teammates will immediately respect.

By the way, a greeting should happen at the end of practice too! Saying things like "Great practice! See you later!" will leave an impression that lasts.

3. Treat Others Fairly and Respectfully

Comparing ourselves to others is something we all do. It's just part of human nature. The trap, though, is that when we make this comparison, it can be easier to try to put down the other person to make ourselves feel better or to try to get ahead.

I've seen this dynamic play out countless times in youth sports. A player who wants more playing time might subtly criticize teammates who play the same position. A student hoping for a leadership role might emphasize others' short-comings. These approaches might seem strategic in the moment, but they actually create the opposite impression from what you want.

When coaches and teachers observe this behavior, they don't see a talented player or student who deserves more opportunity—they see someone who prioritizes personal advancement over team success and creates a negative environment. This impression can overshadow even exceptional physical talent or academic ability.

Part of how to make a positive impression is to show how you're different. Here, we're going to avoid that trap of comparing ourselves to others and instead treat everyone with fairness and respect. This means treating others equally, from the first-string quarterback to the fourth-string quarterback, to the head coach, to the person who turns the lights on in the gym, to the people who close the gates behind you after the game is over. In the classroom, it means showing the same fairness and respect to every teacher, and to every student, whether they're a close friend or not.

I remember a volleyball player named Sophia who was easily the most talented athlete on her team. What made her truly exceptional, though, wasn't her skill but how she treated others. During drills, she would partner with less-skilled players to help them improve. When a teammate made a mistake, she was the first to offer encouragement. She thanked the referees after matches and always helped clean up equipment after practice.

Part of how to make this play a habit is to remember that the message has been around for a long, long time. You may have heard of the Golden Rule: Treat others the way you want to be treated. It's the easiest idea in the world to accept, but not always so easy to follow through with.

But if you can find a way to put yourself in the other person's shoes (shoutout to Chalk Talk #3: Five Plays to Make Empathy Your Superpower), and you can treat them with fairness and respect, others will be drawn to you in a positive way. Coaches will see that you think of yourself as a teammate first, the kind of person willing to contribute, and to help build the team up. If you can learn to treat everyone the way you want to be treated, the benefits will extend into the classroom—and into everything you do in life—as well.

4. Be Consistent

The players who tend to stand out are usually the most consistent. They do all the right things all the time, not just when things are going well for them or when they're feeling up to it. They're consistent with it; they do it all the time because it's traveled the eighteen inches from their mind to their heart to make it become action. Be consistent. Do all the right things all the time.

Consistency might sound simple, but it's one of the most challenging aspects of making a positive impression. It's relatively easy to bring your best self to a single practice or class, but doing it day after day, regardless of circumstances, is what truly sets exceptional people apart.

I once coached a basketball player named Alex who was incredible in games but inconsistent in practice. Some days he would work hard, be engaged, and show leadership. Other days he would arrive late, give minimal effort, and display a negative attitude. Despite his talent, I struggled to give him significant playing time because I never knew which version of Alex would show up.

In contrast, I had another player named Jamal who wasn't as naturally talented but approached every practice with a positive attitude, focus, and work ethic. Whether we were winning or losing, whether he was playing well or struggling, Jamal's commitment and behavior remained constant. As the season progressed, I found myself trusting and relying on Jamal more and more, even though Alex had more raw talent.

Consistency builds trust, and trust is the foundation of any strong relationship—including the relationship between a player and coach or student and teacher. When you're consistent, you become dependable. Your coach knows they can count on you to give your best effort every day, to maintain a positive attitude regardless of circumstances, and to represent the team well both on and off the field.

Building consistency starts with small commitments that you fulfill every time. Begin by identifying one specific behavior you can maintain daily—perhaps arriving ten minutes early to practice, doing five minutes of extra work on a skill you're developing, or sending a thank-you text to your coach after each practice. Once that behavior becomes automatic, add another. Over time, these small consistent actions build into a reputation for reliability that coaches and teachers deeply value.

5. Control What You Can Control

Here we come full circle back to that opening message to control what you can control. We already know that the first two things you can control are being on time and being prepared. What comes next? Well, in sports and in life, it's usually two things: 1) your effort, and 2) your attitude.

When it comes to effort, working hard isn't enough. Whoa! Hold on? What did I just say? Working hard isn't enough? If that's true, then what is enough?

If you're trying out for something, you know that every other athlete is going to work hard. You all have that in common. If you want to make a positive impression on the coach, you need to stand out. And what separates the players who work hard from all the other players working hard? It's not just talent and ability. The ones who stand out are those who do more than is expected.

I call this the "plus-one principle." Whatever is asked of you, do that plus one more. If the coach asks for ten push-ups, quietly do eleven. If the teacher assigns five problems, solve six. This doesn't mean being showy or demanding recognition for your extra effort—it's about consistently pushing yourself beyond the minimum expectations.

During your tryout, see what happens if you go beyond what's expected of you. If a coach asks you to run two laps, you're going to try to run three. Even if you can't make it through the whole three by the time he or she blows the whistle, at least they know in their mind that you're willing to go for that extra lap.

And it's not just about one extra lap! Make this play a habit. Be consistent in how you do more than is asked of you. Every time a coach tells you to do something, do that and more.

Doing more than is expected is also about always giving maximum effort, not just when things are going well, but especially when things are going against you. If you have a setback during a tryout or practice, the way you approach the next drill or play will help determine the outcome. Are you going to let that setback get to you and negatively impact the next drill or play? Or are you going to keep a positive attitude and put in more effort so the setback doesn't happen again?

Your response to adversity reveals more about your character than how you handle success. I once coached a baseball player who struck out in a crucial situation during a game. The next inning, instead of sulking or withdrawing, he was the first one out of the dugout, encouraging his teammates and playing defense with even more intensity than before. After the game, I pulled him aside and told him that his response to that strikeout impressed me more than if he had hit a home run. It showed resilience, team-first thinking, and emotional maturity—qualities that can't be taught as easily as baseball skills.

As a coach, when I see great effort in a player, I know that this player is one who is willing to be coached. Even if she doesn't have the same skillset as another player with a bad attitude, I'm going to give her the edge because she's coachable. I know she's going to work hard and go above and beyond to make herself and the team better. That's the kind of player I want on my team.

The next piece is your attitude. If you want to make a positive impression on your coaches and teachers, then you want to be that person who other people are drawn to. You want to know the best way to show that you're that person? Spread your enthusiasm! If you spend every practice or class finding ways to encourage the people around you, then those people will begin to feed off your positive energy. You will show your coaches and teachers that you are not just a great contributor, but a potential leader as well.

Having a group of players who are enthusiastic and supportive of one another is one of the most rewarding things for any coach. It's also a huge part of what it takes to build a winning team. And since you're working to control what you can control, that enthusiasm can start with you!

Don't Forget the Little Things

Everything you do—each action you take in your daily life—gets you one step closer to your goals. Are you getting up early? Are you prepared to go to school? Are you dressed appropriately? Are your shoelaces tied? Did you brush your teeth? All those little things speak volumes about your character and about the person you are. It's not just about being an athlete or a good student. It's about demonstrating all the qualities that make it clear that you are the kind of person people want to be around.

These little things aren't just surface details—they're windows into your character and habits. When a coach sees you with untied shoelaces, they don't just see untied shoelaces. They see potential carelessness that could lead to injury. They see a lack of attention to detail that might translate to missing important instructions. They see a possible absence of the discipline required for athletic excellence.

Be disciplined in your preparation, your effort, your attitude, with the way you treat others, and with how (and how often) you practice. Do these things and you will make a positive and lasting impression on your coaches, your teachers, and your teammates.

As I reflect on my own experience as that high school football player who missed voluntary workouts, I'm grateful for the lesson I learned. Although losing my starting position was painful at the time, it taught me something valuable that has served me well throughout my life: Impressions matter, and they're formed through consistent actions, not occasional effort or past achievements.

After losing my starting position in football, I had a choice to make. I could blame the coach, make excuses, or learn from the experience. I chose to learn. I recommitted myself to the team, showed up early to every practice, gave maximum effort even though I wasn't starting, and supported my teammates enthusiastically from the sideline. By the middle of the season, my attitude and effort had made such an impression that I earned significant playing time, and by the end of the season, I was starting again—not because I was entitled to it as a senior, but because I had earned it through consistent application of these very plays we've discussed.

Your coaches and teachers are looking for people they can count on—people who make their jobs easier and more rewarding by bringing their best selves to every practice and class. By implementing these five plays consistently, you become that person. You stand out not just for what you can do, but for who you are.

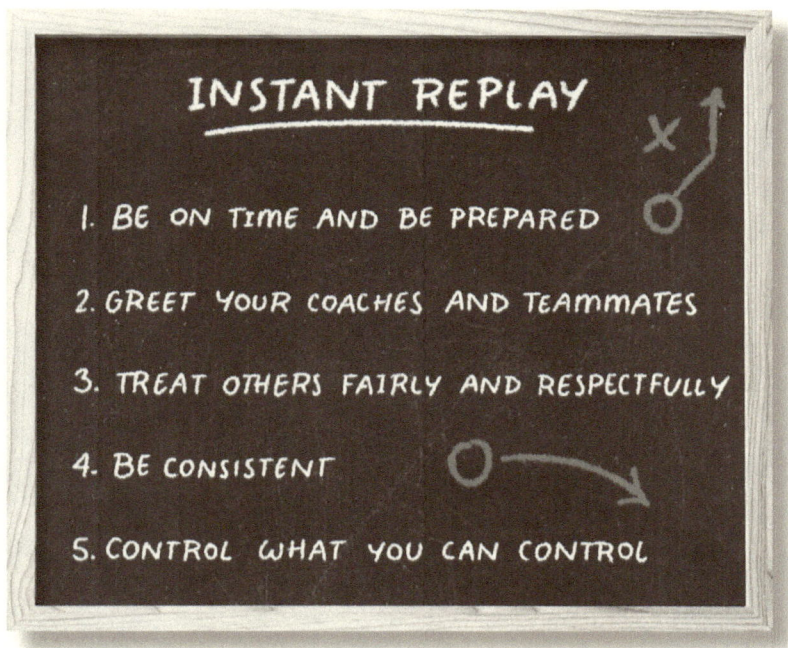

CHALK TALK #8

Five Plays to Help You Grow as a Person Each Day

---

*Any time you have an opportunity to make
a difference in this world and you don't, then
you are wasting your time on Earth.*
—Roberto Clemente

This might sound surprising, but in my post-high school years, I wasn't a very goal-oriented person. I didn't know where I was going, how I could use my talents and skills, and what I wanted to do with my life.

Right around when I turned twenty-five, that all started to change. My best friend from high school, Chris, was an on-the-ball, unbelievably kind person. Everyone loved him, and he loved everyone. As a varsity basketball player who would go on to play college basketball at Westminster College, he wasn't just a playmaker on the basketball court, but also in his school and with his friends.

During that period where I was having trouble finding my path in life, Chris had graduated from college and started a landscaping business that quickly grew into an extremely successful company in the North Hills suburbs of Pittsburgh.

Chris noticed my struggle, and so he asked if I would like to be his roommate. Little did I know that his plan was bigger than just sharing the rent. Chris intended to take me under his wing and help me find my path.

A few weeks after I moved in, he came to me with an idea about how I could put my skills to good use.

"I just learned that the offices on the ground floor of this building are available to rent," he said. "And also the racquet-ball court."

"So you want to play some racquetball?" I joked.

"No, no," he said with a smile. "What if we started a business based out of that space?"

Chris was always someone with big ideas, but I couldn't immediately see what he had in mind.

"What kind of business could we possibly run out of a rac-quetball court?"

He knew me well enough to recognize that sports had been my saving grace, the only consistent positive that had kept me going in life. He didn't need to start another busi-ness—his landscaping company was already successful—but he saw that I needed a spark, that I needed help finding my purpose in life.

"I'm thinking we start a side business where we use the racquetball space to teach kids sports-specific skills. I could teach kids how to dribble and shoot, and all the basketball skills. You could teach them how to swing a bat and throw and catch a football, run pass patterns, all that stuff."

Now he had my attention.

"How much money do you have to start a business like that?" he asked.

At the time, I only had sixty dollars to my name. Like I said, I was having trouble finding my path!

Chris didn't even flinch. "Okay," he said. "I'll match it and we'll get started."

"How do we do that?" I asked, my head spinning about the idea of being a business owner.

First, we decided to call the business Champion Youth Fitness, and then, we put an ad in the *PennySaver*, which was a weekly paper where you could advertise goods and services for sale. I didn't have much money, so our ad had to be something really simple—something like, "Hey, check out Champion Youth Fitness, specializing in sports skills for kids." But we had some good luck, because it turned out that the ad didn't need to be flashy. We were the first business in the area offering to teach kids sports skills. These days, it's amazing how many of those kinds of businesses there are out there, but back then, we were the only game in town.

The day we held our first session was the day I first became Coach Dave and realized my calling in life. And it was Chris who first helped me see that this was the place where my talents would fit. He was a playmaker in the sense that he helped me find my path. He was that one person in life, my guardian angel, the person who said, "Be who you are, with all your faults, and start being that person right now."

One of Chris's many legacies is the lesson he taught me about how growth as a person is possible, no matter where you are in life. With this chapter, I'm excited to pass along the lessons I learned from Chris—and from my grandfather and many other people who have influenced me over the years—on how to grow as a person each day.

Here's the playbook:

1. Don't Take Yourself So Seriously—Find the Joy in Each Day

This first play is one we're already familiar with, but I'm repeating it for good reason: It's just way too easy these days to take everything that someone says or that happens to us too seriously. For a lot of people, it's also easy to forget that sometimes we have to laugh at ourselves, and that the people we meet will always appreciate an effort to make them smile or laugh.

One of my favorite stories to tell at camp is how I once set up a game of capture the flag at a field wet with rain from the night before. I had mapped out the whole field ahead of time, but I didn't account for the fact that there would be puddles. As I was demonstrating how to play, I sprinted across the field and hit a puddle that was much deeper than I thought. I went flying into the air and landed face-first in the mud.

For a moment, all the kids just stared at me in shock. I could have gotten upset or embarrassed, but instead, I just started laughing. I stood up, covered head to toe in mud, and took a bow. All the kids burst out laughing, and suddenly, what could have been a mortifying moment turned into one of the most memorable and fun moments of that camp.

That day taught those kids an important lesson: It's okay to laugh at yourself. It's okay when things don't go perfectly. Sometimes the best memories come from the moments when things go wrong but you find the humor in them.

So at the start of each day, I'd like you to make this declaration: "I'm not going to take myself too seriously today." And at the end of each day, I'd like you to pause and reflect on two questions: "Did I make someone smile or laugh today?" and "Was there a time when I was able to laugh at myself?"

The more you make these declarations and ask these questions, the closer you will get to making this first play a habit of the heart. Remember, life is too short to go through it without finding joy in each day—even if that joy comes from laughing at your own mistakes!

2. Be Your Authentic Self—Real, Sincere, and True to Who You Are

One of the things you might notice as you get older is that some people have a hard time allowing others to see who they truly are. It was definitely a challenge for me in school. I spent so much of my grade school years as an outcast that when I got into high school, I did everything possible to try and make my classmates like me. This meant behaving in ways that weren't true to who I was. And when you're not true to yourself, life can become more challenging. For me, it reflected in my grades, in the friends I kept, and in the choices I made at home and outside of school.

Being real, sincere, genuine, and true to yourself is one of the best ways to make a positive difference in the lives of the people around you. It's funny how this works, but the more honest you are with yourself, the more people will respect you, and the bigger the impact you will make on their lives.

But what does it mean to be real, sincere, genuine, and true to yourself? It means that you think things through before you act. It means that you always do your absolute best to make the right choices. It means that you take responsibility for your actions.

I remember one time when I was working with a group of middle schoolers at a week-long sports camp. There was one camper, Tyler, who was hesitant to participate in activities. He would hang back, not engage with other kids, and I could tell he wasn't having much fun. One day, I pulled him aside and asked what was going on.

"I'm not really a sports person," he admitted. "My parents made me come here."

Instead of trying to convince him that he should love sports, I asked what he was interested in. Turns out, Tyler was really into photography and art. So I gave him a special role for the week—camp photographer. I let him use my camera (with supervision) to document the activities, and he created an amazing slideshow for our end-of-camp celebration.

The change in Tyler was incredible. Once he was allowed to be his authentic self rather than trying to be something he wasn't, he blossomed. The other kids thought his photos were amazing, and he became an important part of our camp community—just in a way that honored who he truly was.

Part of being a playmaker is having the confidence to always be yourself. The goal each day and in every interaction should be to always be 100 percent genuinely you. This means being honest with yourself and about yourself, and accepting who you are. It means being ready and never hesitating to offer your own unique personality.

Are you just like the other kids at school? Of course not! And that's a great thing! As a unique person, you are the only you there is—and that *you* has so much to offer. Share your unique personality and your special skills and talents with the world every day.

Your challenge at the start of each day: Find a moment (or more than one moment) where you can express your true personality in a positive manner.

3. Take Responsibility—Own Your Actions and Your Growth

Before we start thinking about this next play, let me ask you a question. Did you see anywhere in Play #2 where I said, "Being real, sincere, genuine, and true to yourself means that you must always do everything right"? Of course not! Everyone makes mistakes. Sometimes, what seems like the right choice, no matter how much we think about it, turns out to be the wrong one.

When this happens, we have to accept that we made a mistake. We have to take responsibility and ownership for our actions. What does that look like? Well, sometimes, it looks like apologizing. If we have wronged someone, even if it's an accident, it's important that we give a sincere apology. We have to do our very best to be accountable for everything we do, whether positive or negative.

I once had to cancel a birthday party at the last minute because I double-booked myself. I had written down the wrong date, and I didn't realize it until the morning of the party when the birthday child's mother called to confirm some details. I was horrified—I had another event scheduled that I couldn't cancel, and I had no backup coach available.

I could have made excuses or tried to blame something else, but I knew I had to own up to my mistake. I called the mother back immediately, explained my error, and sincerely apologized. Instead of just leaving it at that, I offered to reschedule the party for the following weekend and include some extra activities at no additional charge.

The mom was understandably disappointed, but she appreciated my honesty and my attempt to make things right. After the rescheduled party (which went wonderfully), she became one of my biggest supporters and has referred many other families to my business over the years.

Taking responsibility also means being proactive about your own growth. Chris, my friend who helped me start Champion Youth Fitness, once told me something I've never forgotten: "If you want to get better, you have to seek out knowledge. Nobody's going to just hand it to you."

Can you guess how old I was when I stopped trying to learn new things every day? Trick question! I have never stopped trying to learn. That old saying that knowledge is power is absolutely true. Growing as a person every day requires that you always seek to learn, learn, learn.

So at the end of the day, ask yourself these incredibly important questions: "Did I accept responsibility for my actions today—both the good and the not-so-good?" and "Did I seek to learn something today that will make me better tomorrow?"

4. Serve First—Focus on What You Can Give, Not What You Can Get

One of the most important lessons I've learned in my decades of coaching is that the most fulfilled people aren't those who focus on what they can get, but those who focus on what they can give.

I first realized this during a summer camp several years ago. We had a camper named Mia who had a knack for noticing when other kids were feeling left out or having a hard time. Without being prompted, she would go over to them, introduce herself, and invite them to join whatever activity she was doing. She never drew attention to herself for doing this—she just naturally looked for ways to include others.

At the end of the camp, I asked Mia what her favorite part of the week had been. Without hesitation, she said, "Making new friends and helping people have fun." Not winning games, not being recognized for her athletic abilities (which were considerable), but serving others.

What Mia understood naturally is something that many adults never learn: True happiness comes from serving others first. It's about asking, "How can I help?" instead of "What's in it for me?"

There's a story I love to tell about a man walking along a beach after a storm. Hundreds of starfish had washed up on shore and were dying in the sun. The man noticed a boy picking up starfish one by one and throwing them back into the ocean.

"There are so many," the man said to the boy. "You can't possibly make a difference."

The boy bent down, picked up another starfish, and tossed it into the water. "I made a difference to that one," he replied.

That's what service is all about—not trying to solve every problem in the world, but doing what you can for the person right in front of you. Maybe it's as simple as including kids at recess who aren't being included. Maybe it's packing backpacks for food drives. Maybe it's volunteering with Special Olympics or participating in a buddies program at your school.

Service can take many forms, but it always begins with thinking about others first. Here's a simple way to practice this play: Start each day by asking yourself, "Who can I help today?" and end each day by asking, "Did I make someone else's day better?"

I remember when Hurricane Maria devastated Puerto Rico, where my family is from. A fifteen-year-old boy in one of the hardest-hit areas didn't wait for others to solve the problems. Instead, he organized fundraisers and collected solar light sources to distribute to families without electricity. He didn't say, "I'll wait until we get our power back" or "I'll wait until FEMA comes." He saw a need and took action to serve his community.

You don't have to wait for a disaster to make a difference. Serving first can be as simple as helping a classmate understand homework, volunteering to be a school bus monitor, or picking up trash in your neighborhood park. The key is to look outward, not inward, and ask, "How can I contribute?"

5. Connect with Positive People—Your Support System Matters

We've already discussed what a huge role my best friend and business partner, Chris, played in my life. But he wasn't the only supportive, positive person who helped me become the person I am.

Even as a kid, when I was struggling so much at home and at school, I had a group of three friends who lived in my neighborhood and always brought a positive influence to my days. Every day, after school, we would run home from the bus to put away our book bags, and then we would run out to one of our backyards to play Wiffle Ball or football, or we'd ride our BMX bikes around the neighborhood, or we'd play in our treehouse. On weekends, we'd have sleepovers. These were the moments that, growing up, became the core of who I was. Even during some of the darkest periods of my life yet to come, memories of the positive times I shared with my friends became a saving grace for me. Memories of that positivity at least helped keep me aware of the right path in life, even during those times as a young man when I strayed from the path. Without those memories, I might not have been willing to open up to the help that Chris would later offer me, the help that completely changed my life.

The lesson here is that relationships with positive, supportive people are like your own personal support system. This is why it's so important to think about the impact the people in your life have on you. Who are the people you can always count on to build you up and say and do positive things? These are the people you want to surround yourself with. It's like that old proverb that if you want to fly with the eagles, you have to stop swimming with the ducks.

I learned this lesson most powerfully when I was in my early twenties. I had fallen in with a group of friends who weren't making the best choices. We spent most of our time playing video games, staying up late, and generally not doing anything productive. I wasn't growing, I wasn't challenging myself, and I certainly wasn't moving toward any kind of meaningful future.

Then one day, I reconnected with an old friend from high school who had started a successful business. He invited me to a community service event his company was sponsoring. I almost didn't go—it didn't sound like "fun" in the way I had defined it at that time. But something pushed me to accept the invitation.

At that event, I met people who were passionate about making a difference. They talked about goals and dreams and the future. They were positive and supportive of each other. It was a completely different environment from what I had become used to, and it made me realize how much the people around me had been holding me back—or rather, how I had chosen to surround myself with people who weren't helping me grow.

That realization led me to gradually change my circle of friends. It wasn't easy, and it didn't happen overnight, but as I began spending more time with positive, goal-oriented people, I found myself becoming more positive and goal-oriented too.

So my challenge to you today is to identify all those people that you can be yourself with, the people who like the things you like, the people who support you even in the things they're not as passionate about as you are, the people who always seem to be a part of your most positive memories.

If you have a strong support system full of these kinds of people already, then that's great. But if you feel like you could use a few more people like that in your life, then one of the best ways to do that is to join a club, team, or local organization. Even if it's sometimes challenging for you to try new things, joining a group of people all dedicated to the same goal can be one of the best and most positive experiences life has to offer. If you commit to it, then you'll soon find yourself surrounded by like-minded people who support, encourage, and inspire you to succeed.

The Positive Difference

When I approach each day, I keep in mind a list of small daily actions that I can take to make a positive difference for the people I engage with. The nice thing about this list is that if you practice it for long enough, it's easy to make it a habit. It may take a little while before it becomes natural in every interaction, but no matter who you are, you can master these actions.

Here's my list:

- Compliment as many people as possible over the course of the day.
- Greet at least one person who is outside your circle, someone you wouldn't normally talk to.
- Introduce yourself to at least one new person each day.
- Be sure to thank as many people as you can whenever you interact.

Now, does your list need to look exactly like mine? No way! You are a unique person, and your list should be just as unique. The point is to create a list of small, actionable things that you can do for or say to other people to help spread positivity. Maybe your list could include something like, "Make sure to say hello to my teacher and ask about their day. Tell them that I'm excited for today's lesson." Maybe it could say, "Include someone new into my game at morning recess."

Each night, after you plug in your phone and put it away, sit down and make your list. That way, you're not rushing the next morning to put it together when you could be having fun with your hygiene routine and eating breakfast. Then, keep that list with you and do your best to check off each item every day. Do this for long enough and it will become a part of who you are—and everywhere you go, you will be the kind of person who brightens people's day and makes them feel good about themselves.

The remarkable thing about personal growth is that it's never finished. There's always another level to reach, another skill to master, another way to become better at being you. But the most important thing to remember is that growth isn't a destination—it's a journey. And that journey begins with a decision, travels those eighteen inches from your head to your heart, and becomes a habit of the heart that guides your actions every day.

As Chris taught me years ago when we started Champion Youth Fitness with just $120 between us, you don't have to wait until everything is perfect to begin. You just have to start where you are, with what you have, and be willing to grow a little bit each day.

INSTANT REPLAY

1. DON'T TAKE YOURSELF SO SERIOUSLY — FIND THE JOY IN EACH DAY

2. BE YOUR AUTHENTIC SELF — REAL, SINCERE, AND TRUE TO WHO YOU ARE

3. TAKE RESPONSIBILITY — OWN YOUR ACTIONS AND YOUR GROWTH

4. SERVE FIRST — FOCUS ON WHAT YOU CAN GIVE, NOT WHAT YOU CAN GET

5. CONNECT WITH POSITIVE PEOPLE — YOUR SUPPORT SYSTEM MATTERS

CHALK TALK #9

Five Plays to be an Everyday Hero

True heroism is remarkably sober, very undramatic. It is not the urge to surpass all others at whatever cost, but the urge to serve others at whatever cost.

−Arthur Ashe

You know what was really cool recently? At one of my camps, a young girl came up to me wearing a Hulk fist and a Batman utility belt. It made me think about superheroes and their special equipment—Batman has his utility belt, Captain America has his shield, Superman has his x-ray vision.

But what about the Everyday Heroes all around us? They don't have special powers or fancy gadgets. Instead, they have something much more important: character. Their character is their most important piece of equipment, just like we talked about in Chalk Talk #1.

In this Chalk Talk, we're going to explore what it means to be an Everyday Hero—not the kind that leaps tall buildings in a single bound, but the kind that makes a positive difference in their community, shows up when others need them, and does the right thing even when it's difficult. These are the heroes we can all aspire to be, regardless of our age or abilities.

I've been fortunate to witness many Everyday Heroes in action, from young kids in my camps to parents, teachers, and community members. What they all have in common isn't superhuman strength or the ability to fly—it's the strength of their character and their commitment to making the world around them a better place.

So, how can you become an Everyday Hero in your own life? Here's the playbook:

1. Be Responsible—Make Wise Choices

Did you know that you make thousands of choices each and every day? Some are more important than others, but each of them has a direct result. Some move you forward. Some move you backward. And some give you no movement at all. An Everyday Hero is someone who understands the power of their choices and takes responsibility for them.

I remember a situation at one of my flag football leagues a few years ago. There was a twelve-year-old named Marcus who was one of the most talented players in the league. During a championship game, a referee made what Marcus thought was a bad call that went against his team. Marcus was upset, and I could see that he was about to lose his temper with the referee.

But then something remarkable happened. Instead of arguing or yelling, Marcus took a deep breath, nodded to the referee, and went back to his team. After the game (which his team lost by a narrow margin), I asked Marcus about that moment.

"I wanted to yell at the ref," he admitted. "But then I remembered what my dad always tells me—that I'm responsible for how I react to things that happen to me. I can't control the ref's call, but I can control how I respond to it."

That's what being responsible is all about—understanding that while we can't control everything that happens to us, we can control how we respond. Everyday Heroes make wise choices even in difficult situations. They think before they speak or act. They consider the consequences of their actions not just for themselves, but for others around them.

Throughout the course of the day, you have countless opportunities to make wise choices. Should you speak up when you see someone being teased? Should you tell the truth even when it might get you in trouble? Should you do your homework first or play video games? Each choice has a consequence, and Everyday Heroes understand that they're accountable for those consequences.

Here's a challenge for you: At the end of each day, reflect on the choices you made. Ask yourself: "Did I make wise choices today? Did I take responsibility for my actions? Did I think about how my choices affected others?" This simple reflection can help you build the habit of making responsible choices—a key trait of Everyday Heroes.

2. Show Gratitude—Be Inclusive of Others

Everyday Heroes understand that gratitude and inclusivity go hand in hand. When we're grateful for what we have and for the people in our lives, we're more likely to share and include others in our good fortune.

Let me tell you a story about something I noticed while visiting Puerto Rico, where my family is from. One day at the beach, I was eating some Cheez-Its and spilling a few crumbs in the sand. Two different types of birds were attracted to these crumbs: seagulls and pigeons.

I noticed something fascinating about their behavior. The seagulls would swoop down aggressively, squawking loudly and chasing away any other birds that dared to come near "their" food. But the pigeons behaved quite differently. They shared the space, patiently taking turns and allowing each other to eat. They were opportunistic but not aggressive. They worked together instead of fighting each other for the food.

I turned to the kids with me and said, "Be more like a pigeon and less like a seagull. Be patient. Wait your turn. Be inclusive. When you see an opportunity, take it—but not at the expense of others."

This is a lesson I see play out in sports all the time. At one of my after-school programs, I had a child who was crying at the end of what I thought was a great day. When I asked what was wrong, he said he didn't get to be quarterback enough. He was acting like a seagull—wanting it all for himself, focused on what he didn't get rather than appreciating the fun he'd had playing other positions.

Everyday Heroes are like pigeons—they show gratitude for what they have and make room for others to share in the experience. They understand that when someone else gets something good, it doesn't take away from them. They celebrate others' successes and include those who might otherwise be left out.

One of the most powerful ways to practice this play is to look for kids who might be sitting alone at lunch or standing by themselves at recess. An Everyday Hero sees these situations as opportunities to show gratitude for their own friends by sharing that friendship with someone who needs it.

Try this: Each day, find one person to include who might otherwise be left out. Maybe it's inviting someone new to sit with you at lunch, or asking someone to join your game at recess. Then, at the end of the day, think of three things you're grateful for. This combination of gratitude and inclusivity is a superstrength of Everyday Heroes!

3. Do the Hard Things—Even When You Don't Feel Like It

The hardest part about being a leader and an Everyday Hero is doing the things you don't want to do or don't feel like doing. True heroes tackle challenges head on, even when they'd rather not.

I experienced this myself recently. I had to be at Acrisure Stadium at 5:00 a.m. to set up for a charity 5K race. When my alarm went off that morning, I was tired and worn down. I didn't feel like I had the necessary enthusiasm to make the event special. As I was driving there, I caught myself thinking, "Man, I don't feel like doing this today."

But then I stopped myself and said, "You're being awfully selfish, Coach Dave. I'm not doing this for me. I have to think about the kids I'm serving. The kids who are counting on me to show up and inspire them and motivate them and bring the fun."

Once I shifted my mindset away from feeling sorry for myself and onto doing what I do and being who I am, I knew I couldn't let these people down. And you know what? Once I started setting up and seeing people come in for the race, hearing the positive feedback from the parents and kids, it made it all worth it. It reminded me why I do what I do.

Everyday Heroes do the things they don't feel like doing. They wake up for that early practice. They go to their friend's birthday party even when they're tired. They do their chores around the house. They do their homework. They put in the extra work to learn the plays or study for the test or better themselves. They eat the right things. They read an extra chapter. They go to bed on time instead of staying up late. They put down their screens when it's family time.

There's an old saying that "showing up is half the battle," but that's not really true. It's *how* you show up that matters. It's your state of mind and the energy you bring. As another saying goes, "Don't praise a fish for swimming." You showed up? Good for you—you're supposed to show up. That's the least you can do. Everyday Heroes show up and bring a positive attitude and good energy, even when it's difficult.

Think about it this way: Doing hard things makes you stronger. Just like lifting weights makes your muscles stronger, doing difficult tasks—especially ones you don't feel like doing—makes your character stronger.

Your challenge: Each day, identify one thing you don't feel like doing but know you should. Then do it with a positive attitude. After a while, you'll find that the hard things become easier because you've built the strength of character to tackle them.

4. Lead by Example—Actions Speak Louder Than Words

Everyday Heroes don't just tell others what to do—they show them through their actions. They walk the walk, not just talk the talk. They're doers, not just talkers.

Think about the comic book heroes you admire. When a house is burning and someone needs help, Superman doesn't stand around telling others what to do. He changes in the telephone booth and gets to work. He leads by example, not because he's seeking praise, but because it's the right thing to do.

I witnessed a powerful example of this during a flag football game with fifth graders last season. It was a competitive bunch of kids, and the game was tied until the final minutes when one team scored the winning touchdown. The whole team was running around high-fiving and chest-bumping, celebrating their victory—except for one player.

This player, instead of joining the celebration, went directly over to the other team and said, "Hey, great job today." He took that moment to take the spotlight off himself and his team's victory to acknowledge the hard work and effort of the opponents. It wasn't an empty gesture either; the player he complimented had truly played hard and made an impact throughout the game.

That's leading by example. In that moment, this young player showed more character and leadership than many adults I know. He demonstrated that being an Everyday Hero isn't about seeking the spotlight—it's about shining that spotlight on others.

Leading by example also means being mindful of your tone of voice and body language. How we speak to one another is just as important as what we say. When I work with my Recess Buddies program, I'm always conscious of my tone—making sure it's enthusiastic, positive, and inclusive. "Hey, does anybody have a birthday this week or next week?" I'll ask with genuine excitement in my voice.

For many kids, being enthusiastic for others doesn't come naturally. They tend to lead from an "I" point of view. But

Everyday Heroes understand that their energy, tone, and body language can have a huge impact on those around them.

Your challenge: Pay attention to how you speak to others today. Are you using an enthusiastic tone when talking about their accomplishments? Is your body language showing that you're genuinely interested in what they have to say? Find at least one opportunity today to lead by example—to demonstrate the behavior you'd like to see in others.

5. Compliment Genuinely—See the Good in Others

One of the most powerful tools an Everyday Hero has is the ability to notice and acknowledge the good in others. Genuine compliments can transform someone's day, boost their confidence, and strengthen your connection with them.

I remember going to a school on St. Patrick's Day when everyone was wearing green. I made a point to notice the effort kids had put into their outfits. "That is the greatest green ensemble I've ever seen!" I told one student. The smile that broke out on their face was priceless—all from a simple, genuine compliment.

Compliments are like hidden tools that many kids (and adults too!) don't realize they have. If they knew they could have such a huge impact by simply going up to someone and paying them a compliment—without looking for anything in return—it would transform the way they interact with others.

But here's the key: Compliments must be genuine. Kids can tell when you're just saying something nice without meaning it. The best compliments are specific and thoughtful. Instead of just saying, "Nice job," try something like, "I noticed how patient you were when explaining the game rules to the new kid. That was really kind of you."

Compliments aren't just for special occasions either. Everyday Heroes find something to compliment in ordinary situations. Maybe it's noticing a classmate's neat handwriting, or a teammate's positive attitude even when the team is losing, or a friend's creative approach to a homework assignment.

When you make a habit of complimenting others, you start to develop what I call "appreciation vision"—the ability to see the good in people and situations that others might miss. This kind of vision is essential for Everyday Heroes because it helps them recognize opportunities to build others up.

I've found that the habit of complimenting others has another powerful effect: It makes you more aware of your own positive qualities. When you regularly acknowledge the strengths in others, you become better at recognizing and developing those same strengths in yourself.

Your challenge: Give at least three genuine, specific compliments today. They can be to friends, family members, teachers, or even strangers. Notice how it makes the other person feel—and how it makes you feel too. Over time, try to increase the number of compliments you give each day, and watch how it transforms your relationships and your perspective.

You/Me/We

Before we wrap up this Chalk Talk, I want to share a powerful exercise I use with my teams that brings together many of the Everyday Hero actions we've discussed. It's called the "You/Me/We" exercise, and it's a great way to practice being an Everyday Hero.

During a recent youth running program, I gathered my team together at the end of our session and explained the three parts:

First, I started with the most important piece: the "YOU" part. I said, "I want someone here to point to someone else and say what they did exceptionally well during practice that you noticed and want to acknowledge."

A nice kid named Kenji raised his hand and said, "I want to give a shout-out to Danny. You were running hard the whole time, and even though you weren't at the front of the pack, you never gave up. You stayed with it, and you did awesome!"

Everyone cheered for Danny, and you could see how much it meant to him to be called out like that.

This is the power of the "YOU" part of the picture. Recognizing and celebrating the achievements and efforts of others around you can make them feel seen and appreciated, and that kind of thing is such a big part of what being an Everyday Hero is all about.

Next, I moved to the "ME" concept. I told the group, "When you do something well, it's okay to recognize that too. Can someone here talk about something you personally did well today?"

The group seemed a little less ready to talk about themselves, so I shared my own example: "I felt like my body was giving up physically. My mind was saying that I only had two more runs left in me. But then I traveled the eighteen inches from my brain to my heart, and I told myself I could do four more runs. And I did it! I proved to myself that I can do more than what's required."

This is the "ME" part—acknowledging your own growth and accomplishments without bragging about them. It's healthy to recognize your own efforts, as it boosts the confidence you need to be an Everyday Hero.

Finally, I finished with the "WE" concept. I asked, "Can someone talk about how WE as a group excelled today? What did WE do that was something worth celebrating?"

Danny stood up and said, "I think we as a group were really supportive of one another. When we were doing the drills, I noticed that everyone was cheering everyone on. We were enthusiastic and supportive of each other."

This is the "WE" concept—recognizing how your group or team has come together to achieve something as a unit.

This You/Me/We exercise brings together everything an Everyday Hero does: They recognize and celebrate others' efforts (YOU), take responsibility for their own actions and growth (ME), and understand their role in team success (WE). An important point to think about one more time: The "YOU" part is the most important of all, which is why we start there.

Want to see how powerful this exercise can be? Try it with your family at dinner tonight, or with your friends after playing together. Start by declaring to someone else what they did well (You), then what each person is proud of individually (Me), and finally, what you accomplished together as a group (We). It's a perfect way to practice being an Everyday Hero every day!

The Ripple Effect

When you adopt these five actions of an Everyday Hero, something magical happens. Your positive choices, your gratitude and inclusivity, your willingness to do hard things, your leadership through example, and your genuine compliments create ripples that extend far beyond you.

Think of it like dropping a stone into a pond. The stone

itself might be small—maybe it's just a sincere compliment to someone who's having a tough day—but the ripples spread outward, affecting more and more of the pond. That person you complimented feels better and treats the next person they meet with more kindness. That person, in turn, carries that positive energy forward. Before you know it, your small action has created a wave of positivity.

Every day, in countless small ways, you have the opportunity to be a hero in someone's story. You don't need supernatural powers or a fancy costume—just the courage to make responsible choices, the heart to include others, the strength to do difficult things, the integrity to lead by example, and the vision to see and acknowledge the good in others.

The world doesn't need more celebrities or superheroes with special powers. It needs Everyday Heroes like you, who understand that true heroism isn't about grand gestures or saving the day in spectacular fashion. It's about consistent, daily actions that make the world a little better for the people around you.

INSTANT REPLAY

1. BE RESPONSIBLE — MAKE WISE CHOICES

2. SHOW GRATITUDE — BE INCLUSIVE OF OTHERS

3. DO THE HARD THINGS — EVEN WHEN YOU
   YOU DON'T FEEL LIKE IT

4. LEAD BY EXAMPLE — ACTIONS SPEAK
   LOUDER THAN WORDS

5. COMPLIMENT GENUINELY — SEE THE GOOD
   IN OTHERS

THE FINAL PLAY

U > i

Life's most persistent and urgent question is:
What are you doing for others?
—Martin Luther King Jr.

Throughout this book, we've explored many different plays to help you develop strong character, show empathy, grow as a person, and become an Everyday Hero. Now we've arrived at what I consider the most important play of all—the one that brings everything else together: U > i.

What does "U > i" mean? It's simple but profound: You putting others before yourself. The "U" (you) is greater than the "i" (me). It's about making choices and taking actions that benefit others, not just yourself. It's about shifting your focus from "What's in it for me?" to "How can I make a difference for you?"

This might sound like a strange concept in today's world. After all, we're constantly bombarded with messages about being the best, standing out from the crowd, getting ahead, and focusing on our own success. Social media encourages us to share our achievements and build our personal "brand." Club sports and competitive activities often emphasize individual stats and performance over team growth and cooperation.

I see this every day in my work. When kids come to my camps or after-school programs from highly competitive environments, they often bring that "it's all about me" mentality with them. The spotlight is on their performance, their stats, their achievements. And while there's nothing wrong with working hard and developing your skills, problems arise when that individual focus overshadows everything else.

I remember one camp where a talented young athlete got so upset after his team lost a game that he announced to everyone, "My team sucks!" It broke my heart—not just because it was poor sportsmanship, but because of what it revealed about his perspective. In his mind, the team existed to showcase his talents, not the other way around.

The U > i mindset flips this perspective completely. It recognizes that true fulfillment doesn't come from putting yourself first—it comes from putting others first. It's about understanding that we're all connected, and that your choices and actions affect everyone around you.

So how do we develop this U > i mindset? How do we make it our final play—the one that ties together everything else we've learned? Here's the playbook:

1. Shine the Spotlight On Others

Nine out of ten kids—and adults too, if we're being honest—naturally want all the glory and accolades for themselves. What's much harder to do is to step back, be humble, and give praise and recognition for other people's accomplishments.

I'll never forget the first time I learned this lesson. Back when I was just starting out as a youth sports coach, I was fortunate enough to be invited to watch a practice between two high-level NCAA basketball teams. This opportunity came about through a mutual friend who knew the head coach of the visiting team. This head coach also happened to be an NCAA Hall of Fame basketball coach.

When I arrived at the arena, I was planning to sit back a few rows and just watch quietly. But the legendary coach spotted me and called out, "Coach Dave! Come on down here and sit on the bench with us." He actually invited me to sit at the end of the bench with his players. It was unbelievable.

As I watched the practice from that awesome spot, I was amazed by how the coach pulled everything together. Each player hung on his every word, listening carefully and following every command exactly as he understood it. It was incredible to see how tight of a ship that coach ran and how disciplined his players were.

Toward the end of practice, during a water break, the coach looked down at me and said, "Coach Dave, let me give you some advice since you're starting out in your coaching career."

"What is it?" I asked excitedly.

"If you want to win your players over to your winning philosophy, to your winning culture, if you want to get the best out of them and their best performance, here's what you have to do first."

I was practically shaking with anticipation. "What is it?"

He smiled and said, "You have to make their eyes shine."

You might recognize that phrase, "eyes shine," from back in Chalk Talk #4 about creating a positive mindset. And you're right! This is where that idea came from.

Back then, though, I didn't know what the coach meant, so I politely asked him to explain.

"Every single player on your team or every member in your organization has to know that you see them," he said. "They also have to know that they have a responsibility to the team. They have to know that their contribution is worthy. You have to let them know that you appreciate it, and you have to let your team know that not one player has a greater responsibility or is held in a higher place than anyone else. We're all in this together. No matter what you do for the team, it contributes just as much, whether you're a starter or the sixth player off the bench."

He went even further: "You have to let your players know that what they do matters—whether you're an assistant coach, a trainer, or even the custodian that turns the lights out after everyone leaves."

I never forgot those words. From that day forward, I have made it a point to look for ways to make the eyes shine for everyone I encounter. That's the greatest way to make a connection, and to me, it's also the greatest way to win people over to what you're trying to do as a leader or a team: by making their eyes shine, by taking the spotlight off of yourself and shining it on others. You have to let them know that what they do really matters.

This is what focusing on others first looks like in practice. It's not about ignoring or minimizing your own accomplishments or putting yourself down. It's about understanding that the most powerful thing you can do is help others see their own value and contribution. When you make someone's eyes shine, you're telling them they matter—and that's a gift that keeps giving.

There's another benefit too. When you make a habit of noticing and acknowledging others, something amazing happens: You start to see more *goodness* in the world around you.

It's like developing a superpower of appreciation that helps you connect more deeply with everyone you meet.

2. Listen to Understand—Not Just to Respond

In today's world, it's easy to fall into the trap of waiting for your turn to talk instead of truly listening to what others are saying. When everything's about "I," there's no room for questions like "What about you?" or "How are you feeling?"

Real listening is a cornerstone of the U > i mindset. When you listen to understand, you're saying to the other person, "You matter. Your thoughts and feelings are important to me." You're putting their need to be heard above your need to be heard.

Try this: In your next conversation, challenge yourself to ask at least three questions before sharing your own thoughts or experiences. Not just any questions, but ones that show you're truly engaged with what the other person is saying. "How did that make you feel?" "What happened next?" "What was the most challenging part for you?"

When you practice this kind of listening, you'll be amazed at how much more you learn about the people around you—and how much stronger your connections become.

3. Be Respectful and Mindful of Your Tone and Body Language

Have you ever had someone roll their eyes while you were talking? Or look at their phone instead of at you? Or use a sarcastic tone that made you feel small? These subtle signals can be even more hurtful than the words people say, because they communicate a fundamental lack of respect.

The U > i mindset requires us to be especially mindful of how we communicate—not just the words we choose, but the tone of voice, facial expressions, and body language that accompany them. These nonverbal cues often speak louder than words, revealing whether we truly value the other person or are just going through the motions.

For adults, this kind of enthusiasm often comes naturally when we're excited about something. But for many kids, especially those focused primarily on themselves, it can be challenging to show that same level of enthusiasm for others. Yet learning to do so is a crucial part of putting others first.

Your challenge: Pay attention to your tone and body language today. When you greet someone, do you look them in the eye? When they're talking, do you nod and show you're listening? When you ask about their day, does your tone convey that you genuinely care about the answer? These small adjustments can make a huge difference in how you make others feel.

4. Remember the Details–Show People They Matter

One of the most powerful ways to show someone they matter to you is to remember details about their life and interests. It's how I've built connections with thousands of kids and families over the years, and it's a skill anyone can develop with practice.

Think about how it feels when someone remembers your

birthday, or asks about the soccer tournament you mentioned last week, or recalls that your favorite color is purple. It makes you feel seen and valued, doesn't it? That's the power of remembering details.

This isn't about having a superhuman memory—it's about paying attention and showing genuine interest in others. When you meet someone, make a mental note of two things you can remember about them for your next interaction. Maybe it's their favorite sport, or a trip they're excited about, or a pet they mentioned. Then, when you see them again, ask about those things.

"How was your grandma's birthday party last weekend?" "Did you finish reading that book you were excited about?" "How did your science project turn out?"

These simple questions show that you were truly listening and that you care enough to remember what matters to them. It's one of the most genuine ways to put others first.

And here's the amazing thing: When you make this effort to remember details about others, they're much more likely to remember details about you too. It creates a positive cycle of connection and mutual care.

5. Believe in Something Bigger Than Yourself—Serve Your Community

The ultimate expression of the U > i mindset is serving others without expectation of a reward or recognition. It's about contributing to something larger than yourself—whether that's your family, your school, your team, or your community.

Service doesn't have to be grand or dramatic. It can be as simple as helping a neighbor carry groceries, volunteering to clean up at school, or participating in a community food drive. What matters is the spirit behind it—the understanding that we're all connected, and that by helping others, we help create the kind of world we want to live in.

Recently, I held an event for elementary and middle school kids at a 150-acre farm near where I live. One of the activities was a nature scavenger hunt where I had hidden garden gnomes along the trail—seven of them in total. The activity was meant to be a competition to see who could discover the most gnomes as they made their way through the course.

One boy participating in the event had a physical disability known as cerebral palsy. He wanted so badly to find those garden gnomes, but he couldn't move around the trail as quickly as the other kids.

While everyone else took off running in search of those garden gnomes so they could win the prize, one individual did something remarkable. He teamed up with the boy with cerebral palsy. He would talk him through the course at a slower speed than his peers, keeping engaged with conversation about how they would find a gnome any minute now. Every so often, he would say, "Hey, I'll be right back," then go out and find a gnome. But instead of keeping it for himself, he would bring it back to the boy and present it to him, saying, "Look, you got one! We're a team, so this one is yours."

In this amazing way, that young person took the spotlight off of his own interests and put it on someone else. He gave up his own chance to win in order to make sure another kid in the group could experience the joy of discovery and accomplishment.

I saw that boy with the disability recently at another program I help run, and when he was asked what his favorite part of our year-long program had been, he immediately said it was that end-of-year nature trail scavenger hunt. I knew why—and the kids who attended knew why too.

This is what believing in something bigger than yourself looks like. It's recognizing that we're all connected, and that sometimes the greatest victory isn't winning for yourself—it's helping someone else achieve the same goals and experience the same happiness that everyone else gets to enjoy.

The beautiful thing about this story is that it shows how acts of service can be simple. You don't have to do something grand or dramatic. Sometimes believing in something bigger than yourself is just about helping someone who needs a little extra support, making sure they're included, and showing them that what they can contribute matters just as much as anyone else's contribution.

When we believe that helping others helps ourselves, when we understand that our individual success doesn't mean quite as much if it comes at the expense of others being left behind, we discover what true fulfillment really means.

Your challenge: Identify one way you can serve others this week. It might be joining an existing service project at school, helping out at home without being asked, or simply finding someone who needs encouragement and being there for them. Whatever you choose, approach it with the U > i mindset—not asking "What's in it for me?" but "How can I make a difference for others?"

Small Actions, Big Impact

When you adopt the U > i mindset, something remarkable happens: Your actions create ripples that extend far beyond you. The positivity, kindness, and service you put out into the world doesn't just affect the people you directly interact with—it spreads to everyone they interact with too.

I think of it like this: Each time you put others first—whether by listening deeply, offering a sincere compliment, using a respectful tone, remembering what matters to them, or serving without expectation of reward—you're creating a moment of connection and positivity. That person carries that positive energy forward to their next interaction, and the ripple continues.

In this way, your seemingly small choices can have an enormous impact. The student you include at lunch might go home feeling valued for the first time in weeks. The teammate you encourage might find the confidence to keep trying when they'd been ready to quit. The neighbor you help might be inspired to help someone else in turn.

This is the true power of U > i: It transforms not just individual relationships, but entire communities. It creates a culture where people look out for each other, celebrate each other's successes, and work together toward common goals.

The Final Challenge

As we come to the end of our journey together through this book, I want to leave you with one final challenge: Make U > i your daily practice. Look for opportunities, big and small, to put others first. Not just once in a while, not just when it's easy or convenient, but as a fundamental approach to how you live your life.

This doesn't mean ignoring your own needs or never celebrating your own achievements. It simply means understanding that true fulfillment comes not from focusing primarily on yourself, but from connecting with and contributing to the lives of others.

Remember that this final play—U > i—brings together everything else we've talked about in this book. It requires strong character, genuine empathy, a commitment to personal growth, and the courage to be an Everyday Hero. It travels those crucial eighteen inches from your head to your heart, becoming not just something you know, but something you live.

When you make U > i your daily practice, you become the kind of person others want to be around—the kind of friend, classmate, teammate, and family member who makes everyone feel valued and important. You create positive ripples that extend far beyond your immediate circle. And you discover that by putting others first, you actually enrich your own life beyond measure.

So what will you do today to put U > i into practice? How will you shine the spotlight on someone else? Whose day will you brighten with your full attention and genuine interest? How will you serve without expecting anything in return?

The answers to these questions—lived out day by day, choice by choice—will shape not just who you are, but the world around you. And that, my friend, is the ultimate play.

INSTANT REPLAY

1. SHINE THE SPOTLIGHT ON OTHERS

2. LISTEN To UNDERSTAND — NOT JUST To RESPOND

3. BE RESPECTFUL AND MINDFUL OF YOUR TONE AND BODY LANGUAGE

4. REMEMBER THE DETAILS — SHOW PEOPLE THEY MATTER

5. BELIEVE IN SOMETHING BIGGER THAN YOURSELF — SERVE YOUR COMMUNITY

COACH DAVE GRAY

About the Author

Dubbed the "Mister Rogers of Youth Sports" by parents who know him, Coach Dave Gray brings fun and enthusiasm to his programs, camps, assemblies, and team-building events with his upbeat personality.

With his decades-long commitment to community service and outreach, Coach Dave has touched the lives of youth locally, regionally, and nationally. He believes strongly that instilling confidence and building self-esteem in others is a sure-fire way to become the best version of yourself and truly make a positive impact in this world. Coach Dave's story and impact is not just the story of an individual; it really is a testament to the power and the influence of our educators in shaping a child's future. Coach Dave was in the foster system until he arrived at North Allegheny as a young child. In his words: "I can honestly say, without the teachers and coaches I had as a student, I would not be in the position I am today, gifted with the opportunity to guide and mentor the next generation."

A life-long Pittsburgh resident and 1988 North Allegheny High School graduate, Coach Dave recently celebrated the twenty-sixth anniversary of the founding of his signature youth sports and recreation company, CDG Sports Events. It's not only the young people who attend his programs who benefit from the CDG Sports experience; Coach Dave is a job creator for local teens and young adults and teaches the lessons of commitment, hard work, and professionalism to his employees.

Coach Dave is proud to have received the 2023 North Allegheny Distinguished Alumni Spirit Award and the 2016 KDKA Radio Larry Richert's Hometown Hero Award. He is also a community partner with Allegheny Health Network, raising awareness of the health and wellness needs of the Pittsburgh community.

www.ingramcontent.com/pod-product-compliance
Lightning Source LLC
Chambersburg PA
CBHW021109130626
46554CB00002B/598